Show-Me Atrocities

Infamous Incidents in Missouri History

~~~~~~~~

Larry E. Wood

Hickory Press
Joplin, Missouri

Copyright 2018
By Larry Wood

ISBN: 9780970282996

Library of Congress Control Number: 2018901826

Published by
    Hickory Press
    Joplin, MO

Table of Contents

Preface...4

Acknowledgements...6

1 Rather a Mixed Up Marriage................................7

2 A Remarkable Case of Infatuation......................11

3 A Devilish Temper and Cruel Disposition............23

4 Triple Lynching at Osceola.................................34

5 A Case of Patricide?..40

6 Midnight Tragedy in Lucas Place........................55

7 Whiskey and Bad Women...................................63

8 Do You Think It Safe to Kill Them?.....................75

9 The Little Chloroformer......................................85

10 Turlington Tumbles..93

11 A Fitting End to a Dastardly Career..................103

12 The Death of Lula Noel....................................111

13 Go In or Have Blood..120

14 The Tramp Became a Demon............................127

15 They Want Me to Say Yes.................................133

16 Quiet, Effective Work of the Benevolent Association...141

17 Most Atrocious Crime in Dunklin County History......145

18 A Tragedy of the Tenderloin District..................152

19 A Sunday Lynching at Paris..............................158

20 A Black and White Lynching.............................167

21 The Most Terrible Deed Ever in Warren County........172

22 The Mystery of Pine Flat..................................184

23 For God's Sake Give Me a Chance.....................190

24 Coming to No Good End...................................196

Bibliographic Notes...206

Bibliography...212

Index...215

Preface

Missouri probably saw more than its share of murders and other violent incidents in the late 1800s and early 1900s. Some of these stemmed at least in part from the bitterness that was engendered in the state by the Civil War and that lingered into the years after the war. Some grew out of a rowdy, frontier atmosphere that drew an assortment of outlaws, gamblers, and other ne'er-do-wells to the state. Indeed, Missouri was sometimes known as the "Outlaw State" during the late nineteenth century, and during the early twentieth it often served as a hideout for gangsters like Bonnie and Clyde.

I've previously written about many of these incidents. The murder of the Reverend Samuel S. Headlee in Webster County in the summer of 1866, a crime that was clearly linked to the Civil War, and the assassination of Jesse James, one of the more notorious incidents in the history of America's Wild West, come to mind as examples. The first episode comprises a chapter in my book *Ozarks Gunfights and Other Notorious Incidents*, while the second one is the subject of a chapter in *Murder and Mayhem in Missouri*.

But a lot of violent crimes in Missouri's history could have happened anywhere. Crimes of greed, envy, and passion know no boundaries, and they show us more about universal human nature than about any particular place or state. Although a few of the stories in this book touch on the rancor of the Civil War or the rowdiness of the Old West, most describe crimes spawned not by the circumstances of time and place but by unchecked human emotions like lust, jealousy, greed, vengeance, and racial hatred. Many of the crimes arose from everyday occurrences like lovers' quarrels and family disputes, while few, if any, grew out of gigantic social upheavals like civil war.

Many of these stories are not as well-known as the majority of those I've written about in the past, but that makes them no less interesting. Sometimes the obscure stories are the most curious. Some of these stories are studies in depravity, while others are tales of relatively ordinary people gripped by insane impulses. All of them are Show-Me atrocities, not just because they happened in Missouri but because they show us an ugly side of the human character.

Acknowledgements

Most of my research for this book was done through online resources such as newspaper databases, and I'm appreciative of the fact that more and more primary documents are being made available on the Internet nowadays. It's a lot easier, for example, to look something up on the Missouri State Archives' website than it is to drive to Jefferson City. So, I want to thank not just the Missouri State Archives but all the other organizations that are increasingly making their resources available online.

I still did some of my research the old-fashioned way, though, and I want especially to thank Jason Sullivan and the rest of the folks in the reference section of the Joplin Public Library who fulfilled by numerous interlibrary loan requests.

I owe a thank-you to Will Tollerton of the Vernon County Historical Society for helping me identify where certain landmarks in Nevada were located in the mid-1880s.

Finally, I want to thank my wife, Gigi, for her continued support and for her proofreading skills.

Chapter One

Rather a Mixed-Up Marriage
The Murder of Elijah Slocum and Lynching of
Ewing Tucker

With all the talk nowadays about so-called "fake news" and accusations that modern-day reporters try to pass off opinion as fact, one might think that a time existed in our country's history when reporters delivered only objective, hard news. If so, it wasn't the Civil War era.

In fact, there probably has never been a time in our history, including the modern era, when the news was so tinged by political sentiment as during the Civil War and the years immediately afterward. And in no state were the differences of journalistic opinion starker than in border state of Missouri, where wartime loyalties were sharply divided. Although Southern-leaning newspapers in Missouri were generally suppressed during the war, the divided loyalties persisted into the post-war years and are often reflected in newspapers published during the late 1860s. The story of Morgan County residents Ewing Tucker and Elijah Slocum, as reported by rival Versailles newspapers, is a case in point.

Ewing Tucker married Harriet Lefever in Morgan County in 1844, when he was in his early to mid-forties and she was just a girl of about seventeen. Over the next sixteen years, young Harriet bore the old man five children, while he worked as a farmer to support the family. The Tuckers lived in Morgan, Camden, and Benton counties but always in the same general area where the three counties met along the Osage River.

When the Civil War came on, Ewing Tucker left home to join the Confederate Army, even though he was now about sixty years old. Meanwhile, Harriet stayed home raising five kids. Time passed with no word from Tucker until, according to the *Morgan County Banner*, a rumor finally filtered home that he had been killed.

After learning the news of her husband's death, Harriet soon took her kids and moved in with another old man, Elijah Slocum. Slocum was fairly well-to-do and able to take good care of Harriet and her children. According to the *Banner*, a Republican newspaper reflecting a Union viewpoint, Slocum also treated Harriet better than her rebel first husband had.

Then, in the spring of 1866, Ewing Tucker surprised the folks in Morgan County by showing back up very much alive after four years of absence. He moved back to his old place in the southwest part of the county and took possession of the home. But Harriet wasn't there, because she was living with Slocum at his place not far away.

The *Versailles Vindicator*, a Democrat newspaper reflecting a Southern perspective, was less sympathetic to Harriet's plight than the rival *Banner*. And the *Vindicator* took an even dimmer view of Elijah Slocum, whom the editor said "had appropriated" Tucker's wife.

Tucker set out to reclaim his family the same way he'd reclaimed his farm. Reporting the news at the time, the *Banner* called Harriet's conjugal situation "rather a mixed-up marriage."

The marital crisis was seemingly resolved when Slocum reluctantly acceded to Tucker's prior claim on the woman and Harriet agreed to return to her first husband.

But she was not happy, according to the *Banner*, and she finally could stand living with the callous Tucker no longer.

Sometime during the summer of 1866, she left Tucker and, along with her children, once again took up residence with her common-law second husband. The *Vindicator* placed the blame for her leaving squarely on Slocum, claiming that he "enticed the fickle woman to again abandon her husband."

Tucker tried to get his family to come back home again, but this time Harriet declined to go back. Infuriated, Tucker threatened Slocum's life, but Slocum apparently didn't take the threat seriously, because he owned no firearm and made no effort to get one.

By Wednesday, August 29, 1866, Tucker had, in the words of the *Vindicator*, "exhausted all available means to secure the constancy of his wife" and decided to resort to radical action. Early that morning, he came to the Slocum place and opened fire on Slocum as he was milking his cows. Slocum escaped and ran to the house, yelling to Harriet, "They have shot at me!" and urging her to arm herself with a knife and a club and take refuge in an upstairs room.

Harriet did as Slocum advised, and from the upstairs room, she could hear a commotion below. Soon she saw Ewing Tucker climbing a ladder toward her window. She begged him to call off his attack, and he finally retreated back down the ladder after ascending about halfway up.

Tucker took off on foot, but when Harriet went downstairs, she found Slocum lying dead on the floor.

She immediately gave an alarm, but it took some time for neighbors to gather a posse. That afternoon, they tracked Tucker almost to his house, guided by a peculiar mark left by one of his shoes. Local constable Hiram Shockley then went to the Tucker place and found the fugitive calmly at work a short distance from his house.

Tucker denied his guilt but gave inconsistent answers when asked to account for where he'd been at the time of the crime. Shockley escorted him back to the Slocum place, where Harriet repeated the story of the attack and confirmed that Tucker was the man who had shot Slocum. Because it was now almost dark, Shockley took the prisoner to his (Shockley's) home to spend the night with plans to take him to the county jail at Versailles the next day.

Near midnight fifteen or twenty men with blackened, disguised faces came to the Shockley place. The constable met the mob in the yard, where the men demanded that the prisoner be turned over. Having secured only one other guard besides himself, Shockley was greatly outnumbered; so he tried to reason with the vigilantes. The men he was talking to at the side of the house quickly cut him off, though, threatening to blow his brains out if he didn't shut up.

By now, another part of the mob had gained entrance to the house through the front door. Seeing them dragging the prisoner out, Shockley ran around the house to meet them but realized there was nothing more he could do to stop the mob.

When the gang had gotten a short distance away from the house, Shockley heard several shots, and the next morning he found Tucker dead not far from the Slocum home, the scene of Tucker's own crime the morning before.

At last report, Constable Shockley was making "every effort in his power" to ascertain the identity of the men who composed the mob but with no success.

The two rival newspapers offered decidedly different takes on the lynching and the situation that led up to it. Referring to the murder of Slocum, the *Vindicator* said that "a well-directed rifle ball (had) sent the aged Lothario to a land where wife-stealing is unknown," seeming to suggest that Slocum got what he deserved. The *Vindicator* added that the men who wrested Tucker away from Shockley and killed him were "a band of cowardly assassins." The *Banner*, on the other hand, while lamenting that the law had not been allowed to take its course, was rather satisfied to see the "career of a bad man" (Tucker) come to an end.

Chapter Two

A Remarkable Case of Infatuation
The Murder of Dora Broemser

In the days and weeks just after Charles F. Kring shot and killed Dora Broemser, his business partner's wife, in St. Louis on the night of January 4, 1875, for refusing to leave her husband and marry him, most people thought Kring's claim that he and Dora had been lovers was either an outrageous lie calculated to mitigate his guilt or the romantic delusion of a raving lunatic, and some even clamored for Judge Lynch to take matters in hand. By the fall of 1879, with Kring's prosecution for murder bogged down in continuances and appeals, the general opinion was still strongly against the defendant, but it had evolved to the point that many observers, like the editor of the *St. Louis Post-Dispatch*, were willing to grant that "whether Mrs. Broemser had been guilty of any indiscretions" was not known and never would be "until the judgment day." In early 1882, over seven years after the murder, when Kring's side of the story was published in full in the *St. Louis Republican*, Dora Broemser still had her defenders, but just as many people now tended to believe, like the author of an anonymous letter to the *Post-Dispatch*, that Kring had been a victim of Dora's "cruel deception."

Although opinion was sharply divided about the relative blameworthiness of Charles F. Kring and Dora Broemser, one thing seemed certain in the minds of most St. Louis residents. The crime's element of romantic intrigue and the years of legal wrangling in the courts had made the

Kring case, in the words of the *Post-Dispatch*, the "most interesting and important criminal case" that had ever been tried in the state of Missouri.

As a young man, Charles Kring, known then as Karl, apprenticed to an apothecary in his native Germany and took a course of study at a university to become a fully qualified pharmacist. In 1866, when he was about twenty-one years old, he left Germany to avoid military service and came to the United States. His father, Frederick Kring, had deserted Charles's mother many years earlier, migrated to America, and started a new family. Although the father and son were not on friendly terms, they reunited in Illinois, and the elder Kring set Charles up in the drugstore business more than once during the late 1860s. The ventures repeatedly failed, largely because of Charles's extravagance, but each time financial disaster threatened, his father would help him out.

In the fall of 1869, young Kring married Margaret Recker in St. Clair County, Illinois, but Kring was not happy in the marriage. A daughter named Emma was born to the couple in 1870, and the next year the family moved to St. Louis, where Kring went into the drugstore business on Carondelet Avenue. He was, according to his later story, determined to settle down and make a go of it.

In the spring of 1872, however, the elder Kring withdrew his financial support for the project, and Charles had to sell the store to pay off his creditors. Shortly afterward, little Emma died, throwing Kring into despondency. He and Margaret moved away but returned to St. Louis after Charles fell sick with yellow fever. Upon Kring's return to the city, Jacob Broemser offered him a job as a clerk in Broemser's drugstore at Rock Spring, a western suburb of St. Louis. When Kring assumed the position in September, Broemser introduced him to his wife, Dora, and Kring was immediately drawn to the beautiful twenty-five-year-old woman, although he kept his feelings hidden. Kring claimed, in his autobiography, that Dora later told him that she had been attracted to him at first sight as well.

MRS. DORA C. J. BROEMSER.

Charles Kring from his autobiography.   Dora Broemser from Kring's autobiography.

Dora and her two small children fell ill shortly after Kring came to work for Broemser, and Kring's wife, Margaret, served as their nurse. One night in late October, Broemser's store caught fire, and Kring hurried to the scene to help. However, Broemser, according to Kring's story, prevented him from removing things from the building. Kring and other neighbors suspected that Jake had set the fire on purpose to collect the insurance.

Kring took a temporary job at a drugstore on North Eleventh Street in St. Louis, but after a few days Broemser, who'd received his insurance money, came and tried to persuade Kring into going back into business with him at Rock Spring. Kring refused at first but relented after Broemser sent his wife to personally plead the case.

Dora helped out in her husband's store, and during the winter of 1872-1873, she and Kring were often left alone together when Broemser made trips into St. Louis. Gradually, they fell in love or "became infatuated with each other," as Margaret later described their relationship.

According to Kring's story, Broemser confided that he had indeed burned his store to collect the insurance, and he said he also planned to burn his current one because he had it insured for twice its value. Kring kept the secret, even after Broemser carried through with his plan and burned the second store in April of 1873, because he did not want to disgrace Dora. Kring even agreed to help secure financing from his father, with whom he had reconciled, for a new partnership with Broemser in Illinois. By this time, Broemser had begun to suspect that his wife and Kring had feelings for each other, but he seemed not to mind greatly. Either he naively trusted them not to betray their marriage vows, or, as Margaret believed, he "was trading upon his wife's virtue."

In the summer of 1873, the Krings and the Broemsers moved to Mud Creek (now St. Libory), Illinois, where Kring and Broemser again went into the drug business together. Jake, who, according to Kring, was no sort of druggist himself, again spent a lot of time away from Mud Creek, selling patent medicines throughout the neighboring counties. Kring and Dora, who ran the store together, grew more and more attached, and they finally declared their love for each other and became intimate.

Like Broemser, Margaret also suspected her spouse of being unfaithful, but she would not let herself believe it at first, for she, too, was charmed by Dora Broemser. "I was often very mad at her," Margaret recalled later, "but as soon as we met again, I always became her friend..." One particular time, Margaret caught Dora and her husband sitting near each other on a sofa, but Dora "overwhelmed (her) with compliments" and invited her to come to the Broemser home that evening for a visit. "So great was that woman's magnetic influence," said Margaret, that she accepted the invitation instead of giving Dora a piece of her mind as she should have.

Only when Jake Broemser, apparently exasperated at last by his wife's attentions to Kring, confronted Margaret with a love letter her husband had written to Dora did

Margaret finally leave Kring and return to her parents' home, taking the couple's two-year-old son with her.

Sometime not long after the separation, Kring and the Broemsers moved to Nashville, Illinois. Jake was away on business most of the time, and Kring and Dora, according to Kring's story, lived almost as husband and wife. A female resident of Nashville later confirmed that everybody in the small town knew that an infatuation existed between Charles Kring and Dora Broemser, and some even talked of driving the illicit lovers out of town. But the couple's conduct in public was so exemplary that folks could not help smiling when they met them.

The woman recalled one incident, in particular, in the fall of 1874, when she inadvertently witnessed a love scene between Kring and Dora Broemser through the open blinds of the Broemser home as she was drawing water from a well on the Broemser premises. Kring was sitting in a chair, and Dora, standing behind him, took a braid of her long, black hair and encircled it around his neck as she leaned over to look at him. Kring disentangled himself, jumped up, and started "embracing and kissing her so that I thought he was going to suffocate her," the woman remembered.

Not long after this incident, the Broemsers moved back to St. Louis. Kring went to Chicago but followed Dora to St. Louis in December. She was several months pregnant, and Kring was convinced he was the baby's father. On or about December 12, he confronted Dora, demanding to know whether she would leave her husband and marry him. She would not give him a definite answer and, instead, led him to believe that she was contemplating aborting the child.

Greatly distressed by this turn of events, Kring began to believe that Dora had, after all, only been playing with his affections to get him to go along with her husband's criminal schemes and to provide capital for Jake's business ventures. In a letter dated December 14, he declared his intention to kill Dora if she refused absolutely to leave her husband, and on the last day of December he purchased pistol at a gun shop in St. Louis for that purpose. If Kring could not have the woman he loved, no one else would have her either.

Much of the foregoing, of course, is Kring's side of the story. What we know from contemporaneous reports is that, after receiving a brief New Year's greeting from Dora, Kring penned a letter to her on January 2, 1875, again intimating his intent to kill her if she did not leave Jake. On the morning of the 3rd, he wrote another note to her threatening that they would soon lie in one grave, "for we have laid criminally in one bed," if she did not agree to marry him.

On January 4, 1875, Kring called at the home of Jake Broemser's parents about 7:30 in the evening. By now, Kring's infatuation with Dora was an open secret in the Broemser family, but he was granted permission to take Amanda Broemser, Jake's eighteen-year-old sister, for a carriage ride. The two went to Fifteenth and Mullanphy streets, near Dora's home, and Kring sent Amanda to the house to ask Dora to come out and talk to him.

Dora refused at first but finally consented when Kring repeatedly sent Amanda back to the door. Kring asked Dora to step aside with him, as he wanted to talk to her alone, but after they walked away, Amanda could still hear parts of the conversation, carried out altogether in German. She heard Dora call out, "Oh, Mr. Kring, I am afraid of you."

Later, after Kring assured Dora he wasn't going to hurt her, Amanda heard him demand to know whether Dora would leave her husband and marry him. He said he wanted the question settled once and for all. "You know I cannot marry you," Dora replied. "I have a husband already."

Kring told her that was insufficient and that he wanted a yes or no answer. Dora again replied that she was afraid of him and that she thought he might shoot her if she said no. Kring repeated that she had nothing to be afraid of. Saying that he didn't have a weapon, he threw open his coat and invited her to search him.

Apparently convinced by Kring's indignant challenge, Dora finally said, "Well, no, then," in answer to his demand as to whether she would marry him.

Kring immediately drew a pistol and, declaring, "Then let us both die," he shot Dora in the side. She fell, and he shot her again in the thigh. He then placed the revolver to his own chest and snapped it twice, but it didn't fire.

Kring dropped the weapon and ran. About an hour later he gave himself up at a nearby police station, saying that he had shot Dora.

Mrs. Broemser, meanwhile, was taken inside her home. Two physicians were summoned to attend her, but little hope was held out for her recovery. On January 14, Dora gave premature birth to a baby girl who died shortly after delivery. Two days later, declaring on her deathbed that she had never been criminally intimate with Charles Kring, the mother also died. On the 18th, a coroner's jury reached the conclusion that Dora Broemser had come to her death because of pistol wounds inflicted by Charles F. Kring and that the shooting was deliberate and premediated.

On February 17, Kring waived examination in the criminal court of St. Louis and was indicted immediately afterward for first degree murder. He at first wanted to plead guilty to the charge, but he finally agreed to let his lawyers' mount an insanity defense.

Although "a little maudlin sympathy had been aroused" on behalf of Kring, public opinion was overwhelmingly against him during his early court appearances, as a series of continuances throughout the spring and summer of 1875 repeatedly postponed his trial. Many people felt his attempt to kill himself after shooting Dora had been a "sham" he'd concocted to try to mitigate his crime—that he had somehow rigged the pistol to misfire after the first two shots. And they didn't like the continuances, which they saw as delays in justice.

Interviewed in early August by a *St. Louis Globe-Democrat* reporter at her parents' home in Illinois, Margaret

Kring said she still loved her husband. She largely blamed his troubles on Jacob Broemser, who, she felt, had induced her husband to "take upon his own shoulders the responsibility for crimes which Broemser had committed."

Margaret described Dora as a coquette who "liked to be flattered by gentlemen." Having command of four languages, Dora was "as refined and highly educated as she was beautiful," but she was unhappy in her marriage to the churlish Jake Broemser. Margaret felt Dora was truly in love with Kring but that her hesitancy to leave her husband caused Kring to imagine she was in a conspiracy with Jake to rob him.

On September 20, as Kring was walking back to his seat during another continuance hearing at the criminal court, he picked up a chair and hurled it across a table at Jake Broemser, cursing him as he did so and exclaiming that Jake was the cause of all his trouble. Broemser dodged the chair, and Kring was quickly placed in handcuffs before the disturbance could escalate.

Kring's trial finally got underway in late December, and the defendant remained handcuffed during the proceedings because of his earlier attack on Broemser. The prosecution and the defense agreed on many of the facts of the case but differed in their interpretation. The defense argued hereditary insanity and characterized the murder of Dora Broemser as an act of madness, while the prosecution said the crime was motivated by revenge in response to Dora's refusal to reciprocate Kring's love. Arguments in the case ended on December 24, and on the 27th, the jury found Kring guilty of murder in the first degree. In reporting the verdict, one newspaper said the trial had developed "one of the most remarkable cases of infatuation on record."

The defense's petition for a new trial was denied in early February 1876, and Judge William C. Jones set Kring's execution date for March 24. Kring's lawyers immediately appealed to the St. Louis Court of Appeals, mainly on the basis of the fact that their client had been handcuffed during his trial. The judges on the Court of Appeals bench, citing a long precedent in English law, agreed with the defense argument that the defendant should not have been handcuffed. They said that other arrangements, such as providing additional guards, could have been made to prevent Kring from carrying out another attack. Rendering their opinion on March 20, the justices reversed the verdict of the lower court and remanded the case for retrial.

Two days after the reversal was announced, the St. Louis prosecuting attorney appealed the decision to the Missouri Supreme Court. The high court justices agreed to hear the case, but it took over a year before they finally got around to doing so. On June 25, 1877, the Missouri Supreme Court affirmed the decision of the court of appeals, ordering a new trial.

After another series of continuances, testimony in Kring's second trial got underway on May 21, 1878, but the trial ended abruptly without a verdict when one of the jurymen got sick. Still more continuances postponed the third trial until January 1879. After testimony was taken, the jurors retired to deliberate but could not agree. During the deadlock, one of them was discovered to have lied to the court by saying he did not know the defendant when, in fact, he had been a fellow inmate with Kring at the city jail the previous year. A mistrial was immediately declared.

At Kring's fourth trial in November of 1879, the prosecution offered a deal limiting the amount of time Kring might serve if he would plead guilty to second-degree murder. At his lawyer's urging, Kring reluctantly accepted the deal, but on November 12, when Judge Henry Laughlin pronounced a sentence of twenty-five years in prison, Kring seemed surprised and complained that he had been assured that the sentence he might receive would be no longer than ten years. He told the judge that he never would have pleaded guilty if he'd thought he might have to serve twenty-five years, and he asked to withdraw the plea. Laughlin refused the motion.

Kring appealed the decision, and in March of 1880 the St. Louis Court of Appeals sustained Laughlin's decision not to set aside the defendant's guilty plea. The appeal was then taken to the Missouri Supreme Court, which in July of 1880 overruled the Court of Appeals, saying the defendant should have been allowed to withdraw his plea, and the case was remanded for another trial.

Kring's fifth trial was set for September of 1880, but legal maneuvering continued to delay the proceedings into the following year. The trial was reset for early April 1881, but the *St. Louis Post-Dispatch,* reflecting the frustration of many observers, commented in March that the case was so entangled in technicalities that it likely would never be tried.

The trial, however, did get underway in May. Kring was once again found guilty of first-degree murder, and he was sentenced to hang on July 15. Kring's lawyers again appealed the verdict, but the St. Louis Court of Appeals refused to interfere. On the 14th, however, one day before Kring was set to hang, Missouri Supreme Court chief justice Thomas Sherwood stayed the execution until the full court could hear the case.

In late January of 1882, the Missouri high court affirmed the lower court's decision and set February 24 as Kring's new execution date.

About the same time that the Missouri Supreme Court rendered its decision, Kring's autobiography appeared in the *St. Louis Republican.* Kring briefly detailed his early life but largely concentrated on his relationship with Dora Broemser. He said that he and Dora had been lovers but that she betrayed him in the end.

Reaction to Kring's story was mixed. One anonymous woman wrote to the *Post-Dispatch* complaining of Kring's attack on Dora's character and saying that, if he really loved her as he said he did, he would "shield her and die like a man." Another woman promptly responded that, although she didn't want to palliate Kring's offense, she felt he had already suffered considerably and thought it was rather unseemly to attack him when he was just days away from the scaffold. A third woman, who apparently believed Kring's side of the story, went a step further, largely blaming Dora for what happened. She felt that because of the mitigating circumstances of Kring's case and because of the suffering he'd already endured, he should be released. Yet a fourth woman wrote to the *Post-Dispatch* agreeing with the second and third. She said she was very familiar with the Kring case, not just from having read the newspapers, but also because she lived in the neighborhood where the crime was committed and she had gathered a lot of information from talking to neighbors. "Almost any man," she concluded, "placed in the same circumstances, tempted as he was, enticed by a beautiful woman, one day encouraged by her blandishments, the next day repulsed, until driven to the verge of madness, might in a moment of frenzy have committed the same rash act." Even though his offense was a grave one, she felt Kring had sufficiently atoned for it during his seven-year incarceration and legal battle.

Kring's lawyers appealed to the US Supreme Court, and on February 9, Justice Samuel Miller stayed Kring's execution so that the entire court might hear the case.

In March 1882, Kring began writing an autobiography to be published in book form that would expand on the story previously printed in the *Republican*. During the same month, a reporter visited Kring's estranged wife, Margaret, at her home in Mud Creek, Illinois. Despite Kring's crime and his betrayal of her, Margaret expressed concern for his welfare and said she would consider it her duty to take him back if he were released from jail and wanted to reconcile. As she had done in previous interviews, Margaret still largely blamed Dora for her husband's troubles, saying that Mrs. Broemser had "bewitched" Charley.

In late 1882, Kring took sick, but his petition to be removed from the city jail to the hospital was denied.

In early April 1883, the US Supreme Court, by a slim 5-4 majority, reversed the Missouri Supreme Court's decision in the Kring case. The majority opinion, authored by Justice Miller, cited a Missouri law in effect at the time of Kring's crime that said a person once convicted of second-degree murder could not subsequently be tried for first-degree murder in the same case. Even though the state law was changed before Kring pleaded guilty to second-degree murder, Miller said the old law still should have applied in his case.

The case was remanded for further proceedings, but most observers felt that Kring would now go free, since he could only be tried for second-degree murder and the evidence did not support such a charge.

On April 27, Kring was released on $3,000 bond and removed to St. John's Hospital in St. Louis. Deathly ill, he lingered for about three weeks, dying on May 17 with Margaret by his side. A funeral was held the next day at St. Nicholas Roman Catholic Church, and Kring was buried in Bellefontaine Cemetery. Upon hearing of Kring's death, most people on the streets of St. Louis expressed the sentiment that he had sufficiently expiated his crime. From a legal standpoint, the case was regarded by many as "the most remarkable in the annals of criminal history in this country."

Chapter Three

A Devilish Temper and Cruel Disposition
The Story of Hade Brown and His Forbearing Wife

In July of 1877, when nineteen-year-old Susan Brown left her husband, Hade, and sought refuge at her parents' home near Cairo, Missouri, she did so, according to the 1884 *History of Randolph County*, because Hade had brutally mistreated her to the point that "forbearance ceased to be a virtue."

If, indeed, Susan left Hade because she could no longer abide his mistreatment, she must have had a change of heart, because subsequently she continued not only to tolerate her husband far beyond the point at which forbearance had ceased to be a virtue but also to swear an undying love her him. Even after he had killed her mother and tried to kill her father. Even after he was found guilty of the crime and sentenced to hang. Even to the point that she took her own life four days before Hade's execution rather than live in a world without her "darling husband." In fact, one would be hard pressed to find a woman who ever showed more forbearance and devotion to a wayward husband than Sue Brown.

In early 1876, when Susan Parrish, then eighteen years old, approached her parents, Dr. J. C. and Martha Parrish for permission to marry her sweetheart, James Hayden Brown, the couple had bitterly opposed the match. Hade, as the young man was usually called, was the son of the notorious Bill Brown, who'd killed a man named Penny in 1865 and was then killed by his brother-in-law a few years later for brutally abusing his wife (Hade's mother). After his father's death, Hade quickly developed a rowdy reputation of his own. According to the county history, he was "an unruly, turbulent, bad boy during his whole life, ever ready to shoot, cut or kill whoever or whatever crossed his path, and always boasted of his ability to whip or kill any one who dared to insult him."

But Susan was madly in love and wouldn't listen to her parents. In late April 1876, she and Hade eloped and got married in Randolph County. Soon after the wedding, though, Hade's "devilish temper and cruel disposition was manifested toward his wife."

In the summer of 1877, barely over a year after the wedding, Susan went to her parents' home and appealed to them for protection from her husband's cruelty. Although Dr. and Mrs. Parrish had strongly opposed the match to begin with, they counseled patience and advised their daughter to return home and try to make a go of the marriage.

Susan went back to Hade for a while, but he continued "whipping and otherwise cruelly treating her," according to the county history. On Saturday, July 21, while her husband was at a picnic in neighboring Monroe County, she left home again and came to her parents' house with her infant son to plead with them for help. The couple yielded to their daughter's entreaties, and Dr. Parrish took her, the little boy, and some of her belongings in a wagon to stay with her older brother in Howard County.

On Monday the 23rd, Dr. Parrish made the return trip, accompanied by Sue's twin sister, Sarah. As the doctor and his daughter neared their home, Hade rode up from the opposite direction, wielding a double barrel shotgun. He stopped them in the road in front of the nearby Bennett place and ordered Sarah out of the wagon, saying he didn't want to hurt her. He then started cursing Dr. Parrish and threatening to kill him.

Parrish tried to laugh off the threat. "Why, Brown, you won't shoot me, will you?"

"Yes, I will, damn you. I intend to kill you right here."

Brown fired the first barrel of his gun, and the blast sprayed the doctor's face and left side with shot. As Parrish tried to get out of the wagon, Brown fired again, discharging the contents of the other barrel into the doctor's right side, and Parrish fell from the wagon. He immediately rose and walked to the Bennett house, and a young man who'd witnessed the scene raced to the nearby Parrish home to tell the doctor's wife what had happened. Brown, having fired out both barrels of his gun, momentarily fled the scene as well.

Brown soon returned with his shotgun reloaded and started "prancing around and making threats," according to Mrs. Bennett. He said he was going to finish Dr. Parrish and tried to get in the house "but did not try very bad."

Before Brown could make good on his threat to finish off Parrish, the doctor's wife, Martha, approached in a wagon driven by her servant. The Parrishes' youngest daughter, Lutie, was also in the wagon. Brown was sitting on horseback near the lane in front of Bennett's house still threatening to kill Dr. Parrish for taking off his wife and baby when he looked up and saw the approaching vehicle. "Here comes the damned old bitch now," he said to Mr. Bennett. "I'll go and give her a couple of loads."

"You wouldn't shoot an old woman," Bennett said.

"Yes, I'll finish her," Brown snarled as he rode off toward the wagon. Flourishing his shotgun, he dismounted and yelled to the driver, "By God, stop that wagon."

The wagon halted, and Mary Osborne, a married daughter of the Parrishes, rushed over in time to hear Brown threaten to kill her mother. Brown ordered Martha out of the wagon, and she begged him not to shoot. When Mary also began pleading with him, Brown threatened to kill her, too, if she didn't hush up.

Martha got down and walked toward the head of the mule team that was pulling the wagon, then started back as though trying to keep the wagon and team between her and Brown. But she raised up as she retreated, and he shot her in the neck. She rested her head on a wagon wheel, and Lutie called for Brown not to shoot anymore.

"Oh, by God, she ain't dead yet," Brown sneered.

Martha took off running, but Brown followed and shot her again when she came to a fence. After threatening to kill several other people, including his mother, his wife, and Mary Osborne, Brown mounted up and took off.

Mrs. Bennett came running to help, but Martha died within a few minutes. It was thought at first that Dr. Parrish's wounds would prove fatal as well, but he eventually recovered.

A posse of men from the neighborhood where the crime was committed caught up with Brown several miles north of Cairo, but they drew back when he threatened to shoot the first one who approached him. They let him escape and soon lost track of him altogether, although it was thought he was headed for Iowa.

He was finally located and arrested at Rochester, Minnesota, in the spring of 1878 after a young man who'd known him in Missouri recognized him on the street and turned him in. He was brought back to Randolph County in early June and shortly thereafter moved to St. Louis for safekeeping. At his arraignment in Randolph County in July, he pleaded not guilty, and his case was continued until the January 1879 term. He was then taken back to St. Louis to await the trial date.

The trial got underway in the Court of Common Pleas at Moberly on Monday, February 10, 1879. Brown's attorneys put up a defense of emotional insanity, or what one newspaper called "the old, old dodge." Their client, they said, could not remember a thing about the crime.

During the first week of the trial, the editor of the *La Plata Home Press* from neighboring Macon County visited

Brown in the hotel room where he was held while court was not in session. The newspaperman found Brown playing cards with his guard, while his wife, Sue, sat behind him on a bed with her arm around his neck.

Brown, opined the editor, "is a fine specimen of physical manhood.... It is only in his conversation and the bullying twang that he gives it that he betrays the coarseness of his nature and his likeness to his father.

"His wife is in court daily," continued the newspaperman, "with her little two-year-old baby boy, courting the sympathy of strong-minded men, while Hade, with his splendid appearance and nonchalant air, is capturing the women who attend the trial in large numbers."

The presence of Sue and her little child in the courtroom might, indeed, have swayed observers, because, although the testimony was "very strong against him," Hade's case ended in a mistrial on February 19 when the jury, reportedly split six for conviction and six for acquittal, could not agree after "four ineffectual attempts" to reach a verdict.

After the trial, Brown was taken to Huntsville and lodged in the Randolph County Jail. However, in mid-March he was again escorted to St. Louis because officials feared "he might be taken from the Huntsville jail and introduced to a coiled hemp patch." In addition, he'd recently sawed some of the bars of his cell window in two and was about ready to make his getaway when the escape attempt was discovered.

After the mistrial, some observers thought it might be impossible to impanel another jury in the Brown case in Randolph County because nearly everybody had formed an opinion on the defendant's guilt or innocence. Then in June, Mary Osborne, one of the main witnesses against Brown, died, further complicating the prosecution.

Nevertheless, a new trial was set for the December 1879 term in the Court of Common Pleas at Moberly. In mid-December, just as the trial was getting underway, Brown attempted suicide by swallowing strychnine. Although he

survived, he went into convulsions and became so sick that
the trial had to be postponed. It resumed on December 29 but
again had to be postposed when one of the jurors took sick.

When the trial finally got underway for real in late
January 1880, Judge G. H. Burckhartt overruled a defense
motion to recuse himself on account of prejudice, and he also
rejected a motion for a change of venue. Commenting on the
latter motion, the *Home Press* editor allowed that there was
indeed "a bitter prejudice against Brown in Randolph
County, not only on account of the heinous crime for which
he is being tried," but also because of his "reckless and
dissolute life" prior to the murder and his father's reputation
as a "desperate and quarrelsome man," who had killed a
"good citizen of Randolph County" and was "the hero of
many shooting affrays." A lot of the ill-will against the
father, the newspaperman concluded, had been "visited upon
the son."

Brown did little to lessen the prejudice against him
when, during the second day of testimony, he exploded at
David King, one of the witnesses against him, exclaiming
that King was swearing to a lie. Rising to a fighting position,
Brown was seized by the bailiffs, and it took "four or five
strong men to hold him," according to the *Home Press*, as he
"seemed to be endowed with the strength of a giant." Brown,
who had been subject to periodic fits ever since taking the
strychnine, "foamed at the mouth and seemed to be affected
by a strong paroxysm."

Among the pieces of evidence Brown's lawyers
presented in their pursuit of an insanity defense was a letter
their client had written to his wife purporting to show his
fragile state of mind:

> I died for the love of my wife and child. I hope that the
> Lord may bless them. Dear Susan, I died for the way you done me.
> I done you wrong, but I hope you will forgive me. A kiss for
> you and the baby—kiss him every day for his dying father, who
> never will see him again and hope to meet him in heaven.
>   Dear Susan, look on this every day, don't destroy it. Dear
> wife, I hope that you may have pleasure in this world. Please

don't try to learn my child to damn his father. Show him my picture and tell him who I am. This is my dying words. Kiss my picture yourself. I love you better than I ever did, but that does no good now. Goodbye. A dying kiss to my child and Susan, too.

The case was given to the jury on February 4, and they came back after deliberating only about fifteen minutes with a verdict of guilty of murder in the first degree. On February 9, Judge Burckhartt overruled a defense motion for a new trial and pronounced a sentence of death by hanging on March 26. An appeal to the Missouri Supreme Court, however, stayed the execution.

Shortly after sentence was pronounced, Brown was taken to St. Louis but was turned away when he had a seizure upon his arrival. The St. Louis authorities did not want to incur the extra medical expenses to take care of him, and he was escorted back to Huntsville and lodged in the Randolph County Jail.

A week or so later, a correspondent of the *St. Louis Republican* visited the prisoner at the jail in Huntsville. Brown complained of the prejudice against him in the Randolph County area and the unfair treatment he'd received at his trial. He admitted that his father "had a fuss with a fellow named Penny" one time, but he claimed that he himself was "never interested in a fight" since he was born. He complained of headaches but said he hadn't taken poison, vehemently denying the insinuation that Susan had supplied him with strychnine. "My wife would be the last person to ever give me anything of that kind."

In late March, Brown was moved to Kansas City for safekeeping.

In early May, the Missouri Supreme Court handed down its decision affirming the lower court's verdict in Brown's case. Among the defense exceptions were claims that Brown was insane, that he should have been granted a change of venue on account of prejudice against him, and that the Moberly Court of Common Pleas had no jurisdiction in the case, since the law establishing the court was unconstitutional. The high court rejected all the defense arguments and set Brown's new execution date for June 25, 1880.

A few days after the ruling, a *Kansas City Journal* reporter visited Brown in his cell to get the prisoner's reaction to the news. Brown admitted he "was greatly affected by the news," but he was anxious to correct a report previously published in the *Kansas City Mail* that he had cursed and carried on when he first learned of the high court ruling and had said that he did not want to see his wife and child and would do as he pleased concerning religion. "Now these statements are all untrue," Brown said. "God knows I do want to see my wife and child, and will see them, for I have telegraphed for them." He also said he'd consulted with a priest and planned to be baptized and join the Catholic Church.

Asked about the murder of Mrs. Parrish, Brown told the reporter, "I don't know any more about that murder than you do, and can't recollect a thing about it more than if it had never happened."

Brown said he'd never gotten along with Dr. Parrish but that he'd never had any particular argument with his mother-in-law. He must have killed Martha Parrish, he said, because whiskey had injured his brain, and he blamed his drinking on his "wife's relations."

At the close of the interview, Brown reiterated his desire to see his wife and drew out a small tintype of her. He showed it to the reporter and then burst into tears as he gazed tenderly at it.

Brown did indeed get to see his wife. As his date with death approached, Sue came to Kansas City with her little boy and took a room in the home of Mrs. Belle Fisher so that she could be near her husband, and she began paying him regular visits at the Kansas City jail. For some time, Hade had been vowing to cheat the gallows by finding a way to kill himself rather than let the authorities hang him, and he

Hade and Susan Brown and child. *Courtesy Nancy Meadows and Find a Grave.*

enlisted Sue to help him carry out the scheme. But somewhere along the line Sue made up her mind not just to help her husband kill himself but also to take her own life at the same time. On June 21, she visited Hade at the jail and slipped him a small packet of morphine. (Another report said arsenic.) After confirming the suicide pact, the couple kissed each other goodbye but without any unusual show of emotion or sign that anything was out of the ordinary.

Returning to Mrs. Fisher's house, Sue ate supper with the family as usual and then took her three-year-old boy to a neighbor's house. She came back to Mrs. Fisher's, wrote two suicide notes, lay down on the bed in her room, and shot herself in the head with a pistol. She died instantly.

In one letter, pinned to the dead woman's dress and addressed mainly to Mrs. Fisher, Sue instructed the other woman to please notify Hade immediately of her death. "Please see that Hade's relations take me to Sundell graveyard and bury me with my dear husband, and in the same grave and coffin," the note continued. "These are my dying words, goodbye forever and ever. Please see that my child is raised right, no matter who takes charge of him."

In the second note, found in a bureau drawer, Sue declared, "My darling husband and I will both die tonight. My life is a misery to me for I know that James is to hang, and I am very near crazy over my troubles, they are more than I can bear.... I love my dear husband better than the whole world, and he can't live and I won't—we will both die together."

The notes alerted authorities to the suicide pact, and several officers went to the jail and quietly approached the prisoner's cell. When one of them called nonchalantly for Brown to come to the front of his cell, he looked up and, seeing the gathered officers, knew something was afoot. He snatched the packet of morphine from his pocket and crammed it into his mouth. Before he could swallow it, the officers seized him, and a terrific struggle ensued. "The baffled wretch floundered and fought with the desperation of a madman," said the *Kansas City Times.* "His blasphemies and oaths and imprecations were too terrible for recital in a public print.

'Kill me, you dogs of hell!' he shrieked. 'I've got to die anyway next Friday, and I might just as well die here and now.'"

The lawmen finally succeeded in prying the prisoner's mouth open and pulling out the package of poison. He was then placed under heavy guard.

Although Sue's notes made it apparent that she and Hade had agreed on a suicide pact and Hade's desperate attempt to swallow the morphine when the officers showed up seems to confirm his intent to kill himself, some observers opined that Hade never meant to carry out his end of the bargain and had betrayed his wife both in life and in death. He had, according to the *St. Louis Post Dispatch*, "duped a brave and true woman to death, a woman that was a thousand times too good for a cowardly, treacherous assassin as he."

Despite its praise of Sue Brown as a "true and brave woman," the *Post-Dispatch* added with a note of cynicism that her devotion to her husband was hard to understand, and "as Mrs. Brown was a fool, her taking off will not interfere with the motion of the spheres."

Hade Brown was transferred from Kansas City to Huntsville on Thursday, June 24, 1880. About noon the next day, he was transported from the Randolph County Jail to the scaffold, which had been erected in a pasture about a mile east of the courthouse. A gaping crowd estimated at close to 15,000 watched as Brown mounted the steps with a firm step. Sheriff Nicholas Matlock asked Brown whether he had any final words, and he took the opportunity to address the crowd at some length. He professed religion and admonished any young people present not to follow in his footsteps. He asked for forgiveness and said that he forgave all those who had wronged him. "I am going to meet my dear, sweet wife, who died for me. She loved me better than all the world. They say I put her up to it, but as my God in Heaven knows, I never did it, and knew nothing of it."

After Brown finished speaking, a deputy sheriff read the death warrant, and the final preparations were made. At approximately 1:30 p.m., Sheriff Matlock sprang the trap, and Brown fell to an almost instant death with a broken neck.

The body was cut down after about twenty minutes and turned over to relatives. It was placed in a double coffin and taken to the train depot. When the train carrying Sue's body, which had been preserved and held in Kansas City, arrived, Hade's body was placed on the same train. At Moberly, Sue's body was placed in the same coffin as Hade's, according to the couple's wishes, with their arms around each other in an embrace and a bouquet of flowers between them. They were then shipped on a train to Madison in Monroe County and were buried the next day at Swindell Cemetery about four miles south of Madison.

Chapter Four

Triple Lynching at Osceola
A Burlesque on Officers, Judge and Jurors

In the spring of 1880, St. Clair County, Missouri, had been plagued by an outbreak of crime stretching back several years, and, in many instances, the perpetrators had not been brought to justice because of continuances and other legal maneuvering. All observers, including the editor of the *Osceola Sun,* seemed to agree on this "lamentable fact," but opinions on what to do about the situation varied widely. While most citizens, including the *Sun* newspaperman, counseled "a faithful and rigid enforcement of the laws," others decided that the time for relying on the law had passed. On Wednesday, May 12, the *Sun*'s rival newspaper, the *Osceola Voice of the People*, editorialized, "When murderers go unwhipped of the vengeance of outraged justice, we say emphatically that it furnishes more than the shadow of justification for the people taking the law into their own hands and meting out its righteous and deserved penalties upon transgressors."

Apparently this quasi-official stamp of approval on mob violence was just the nudge the vigilantes of St. Clair County had been waiting for. Because that very night, about half past midnight, a mob of about fifty armed and masked men broke into the St. Clair County Jail at Osceola, dragged three men who'd been charged with murder out of their cells, and hanged them from trees just south of town. The Moderators, as the vigilantes called themselves, left a note at the scene of the lynchings saying they were "tiard of the tardiness of the law" in the administration of justice, and they promised that future murderers and horse thieves of St. Clair County would be dealt with in similar manner.

The people of St. Clair County had a history of meting out summary justice. In late June 1871, Jacob Fleming, who'd shot and killed another man in a saloon a couple of weeks earlier, was dragged from the county jail and strung up when it was learned that his case was about to be transferred to another county. (See the author's *Yanked Into Eternity: Lynchings and Hangings in Missouri.*) Afterward, citizens held a mass meeting and adopted a resolution fully endorsing the mob action.

The lynching of Fleming seemed to deter violent crime in St. Clair County for a while. Between 1875 and 1880, however, several murders and other serious crimes occurred, and the perpetrator often went free. As a result, mob fever once again began to flicker, and it would soon roar into a full-blown contagion.

In January of 1880, eighteen-year-old Chesley Pierce killed William Bohon at a school house three miles east of Osceola. Pierce was arrested on a murder charge and placed in the St. Clair County Jail, and John Parks was also tossed in jail as an accessory to the crime. In April, twenty-year-old John Smith killed William Triplett near Johnson City over an old grudge, and Smith was arrested and placed in the clink with Pierce and Parks.

By mid-May, Pierce and Parks had already been indicted for murder and were scheduled for trial at the May term of the St. Clair County Circuit Court, while Smith was awaiting the action of a grand jury. Despite the fact that the county prosecutor was under indictment for malfeasance in office, the wheels of justice were still turning in St. Clair County.

But apparently not rapidly enough to suit some.

And a little encouragement from the editor of the *Voice of the People* was all the prodding the malcontents needed.

May 12 was a warm day in Osceola, and most folks retired early, according to the *Sun*, "little dreaming that a dark and terrible tragedy would be enacted in the town...before the morning light again dawned." But in the wee hours of May 13, a company of armed and masked men gathered at the St. Clair County Jail in Osceola and called for the guard, Tom Emerson, to hand over the keys. Emerson refused, and after parleying with him for a few minutes, the mob finally resolved to break down the doors.

One man covered Emerson with a pistol, while the others went upstairs and smashed open the outer door to the jail. The vigilantes then turned their attention to the cells, where Pierce, Parks, Smith, and one other prisoner, William Gilbert, were being held. Using sledgehammers, the horde of men made quick work of the locks and soon were in among the prisoners. Pierce and Parks were taken from one cell without resistance, while Smith struggled mightily as he was dragged from the other. Meanwhile, Gilbert, who was incarcerated on a larceny charge, hid in a dark corner of Smith's cell and was overlooked by the mob.

The vigilantes placed ropes around the necks of their three captives and led them downstairs and outside. The mob marched the three prisoners a couple of blocks to Fourth and Chestnut, where Smith made a break for freedom. The vigilantes yelled for him to halt, but he ignored the order and was riddled with bullets.

Taking the Humansville Road to the eastern outskirts of town, the vigilantes marched Pierce and Parks to a grove of locust trees in an area known as Happy Hollow, dragging Smith's body along with them. The live prisoners were strung up to a limb of one of the trees, while Smith's body was tied to the trunk of a different tree.

After the multiple lynching, the mob rode off in a southerly direction, and the victims were left suspended until after daylight on the morning of the 13th. They were then taken down and removed to the courthouse, where a coroner's inquest was held. The jury reached the predictable verdict that the three men had come to their deaths at the hands of parties unknown. After the inquest, Pierce, having no relatives in the area, was buried in the Osceola Cemetery, while the bodies of Parks and Smith were turned over to their families for burial.

The mob action was soundly and swiftly denounced in the local and regional press. Calling the lynchings a "burlesque on officers, judge and jurors," the *Osceola Sun* lamented the "shame, disgrace and humiliation" that had fallen on St. Clair County because of the "murder of three helpless prisoners by a mob," and the editor predicted that it would take years for the county to recover from "the injury brought on it by the ill-advised, murderous transaction of Wednesday night of last week."

Even the *Voice of the People*, which had previously seemed to incite the vigilantes, hopped on the bandwagon of indignation. "Mob law," said the editor, "should be discountenanced by every good citizen as unwarrantable at all times, as a dark, shameful reflection upon the intelligence of the people of our county, and an outrage upon justice."

The editorial criticism of the mob did not go unanswered, however. The vigilantes left two letters near the scene of the lynchings justifying their action and requesting that the letters be published in local newspapers. The missives were picked up on Thursday afternoon following the lynchings and published in the *Sun* the next week.

One of the letters claimed that St. Clair County had been "blindfolded by affidavits…, choked by legal tecknicalities…," and "thwarted by corrupt judges and attornies," making justice impossible to attain through legal means. The writer assured readers that the vigilantes were only interested "in breaking the necks of murderers and thieves" and that law-abiding citizens had nothing to worry about. The letter was signed, "St. Clair Co. Vigilants."

The second letter asserted that the vigilantes were "tiard of the tactics in law…, tiard of the tardiness of the law…, tiard of the expenses…," and "tiard of seeing money buy the criminal from justice." After enumerating a list of crimes and criminals that had gone unpunished, the letter concluded that, far from being a bane to St. Clair County, the lynchings would likely be a boon, because an assurance to prospective residents that crimes would be promptly punished in the county "is the best emigration society that we know of." The letter was signed, "E pluribus Unum."

A third letter was received through the mail by the editor of the *Voice of the People* and published in the next edition of the paper. The letter explained that the vigilantes had "done the work" for "the benefit of the honest people of St. Clair County." The missive concluded, "The law is not any account, and we propose trying Mob Law." It was signed by the "Moderators."

Not only was editorial criticism of the Osceola triple lynching swift and widespread, but Missouri governor John S. Phelps was also quick to respond to the outbreak of lawlessness. On May 17, three days after the lynchings, Phelps, calling attention to the fact that the local prosecutor was under indictment for corruption, issued an order instructing Missouri adjutant-general E. Y. Mitchell to proceed to St. Clair County at once and act as a special prosecutor to investigate the murders of Pierce, Parks, and Smith and bring the perpetrators to justice.

Mitchell arrived in Osceola a day or two later, and St. Clair Circuit Court judge John D. Parkinson, acting at Phelps's request, made Mitchell's appointment as prosecutor in the case official. A grand jury convened on the 20th to investigate the lynchings, and Jack Barker, Decatur Grimes, and Hiram Curry were arrested two weeks later as alleged participants in the mob action. At the order of Judge Parkinson, the case was then transferred to Henry County, and the three prisoners were escorted to the jail in Clinton on June 6 to await the action of a Henry County grand jury. Grimes and Curry were released on bond three days later, while Barker, as an alleged ringleader of the mob, was retained in custody.

Four other men; Isam Baily, Ephraim Baily, Cal Hartly, and W. D. Harryman; were later arrested as alleged members of the Osceola mob, and they, too, were turned over to Henry County. All seven men were indicted for murder under Parkinson's jurisdiction, but the judge who took over the case in Henry County shortly afterward ordered them released on a writ of habeas corpus filed by one of their lawyers. All attempts to prosecute the case then ceased. St. Clair County subsequently sued Henry County to try to get reimbursed for expenses incurred in the initial prosecution of the case, but the Missouri Supreme Court ruled in favor of Henry County.

Thus, another outbreak of mobocracy in Missouri went unpunished.

Chapter Five

A Case of Patricide?
The Murder of Dr. Perry Talbott

After Dr. Perry H. Talbott was shot and killed on the night of Saturday, September 18, 1880, near the small community of Arkoe, about seven miles south of Maryville, Missouri, his sons, twenty-one-year Albert P. "Bud" Talbott and sixteen-year-old Charles Edward Talbott, reported that an unknown assassin had fired the fatal shot through an open window. Suspicion mounted throughout the next month, though, that the sons had murdered their own father, and they and a twenty-one-year-old accomplice named Henry Wyatt were arrested for the crime in late October, largely on the word of a detective who said the brothers had confessed the patricide to him. The Talbotts' case was severed from Wyatt's, and at their trial in January of 1881, Wyatt testified against the two young men. The defense countered that Wyatt himself was to blame for the crime, but the brothers were convicted and sentenced to hang. Even after the Missouri Supreme Court affirmed the verdict in late April, Bud and Ed clung to their story that Wyatt was responsible for their father's death, but in early July, as their date with death neared, Ed broke down and confessed that he had killed his father because he was beating and kicking his mother. Bud confirmed the truth of his brother's statement, as far as he knew it, saying he'd previously kept silent to protect his brother and the family name, even if it meant his own life. But not everyone believed Ed's confession, and just a day or two before the brothers were scheduled to hang, they retracted their statements, once again blaming Wyatt for their father's death, as well as implicating a kinsman named Wilford Mitchell. Even as the Talbott brothers mounted the scaffold and plunged to their deaths on July 22, 1881, many observers still doubted their guilt or at least wondered whether their degree of culpability warranted the death penalty. Among those familiar with the case, it's a question that lingers to this very day.

Immediately after the shooting, Wyatt, the Talbotts' hired hand, hurried into Maryville with the news. P. H. Talbott was not only a physician but also a former state representative and an editor of a Greenback Party newspaper. He was considered one of the most prominent citizens in Nodaway County, and word of his shooting threw the town "into an intense excitement." Investigators rushed to the scene of the crime to see the critically wounded victim and learn what they could about the incident.

They found the doctor lying in bed at his home still clinging to life. Asked who had shot him, Talbott, referring to his strong support for the Greenback Party, offered a vague, mysterious opinion: "Some enemy of the great cause which I have been advocating—or some emissary sent out by the National banks, or some person who has a personal spite at me. I am dying, and do not wish to cast suspicions on any one."

Bud's story was that his father came home from a house call about nine o'clock Saturday night and entered the sitting room, which also served as a bedroom for the doctor and his wife. Bud's mother, Belle Talbott, was already lying down, and as soon as his father sat on the edge of the bed, an unknown assassin outside the house fired a shot through a window. The ball passed through one of the lower panes and struck Dr. Talbott in the side just below the nipple. It passed entirely through his body and grazed Mrs. Talbott's ankle, slightly wounding her, before lodging in the wall beyond.

Headline from *St. Joseph Weekly Herald* announcing Dr. Talbott's murder.

Dr. Talbott sprang up, exclaiming that he'd been shot, and then fell to the floor. Bud ran to his father's aid and helped him into bed. He then picked up a shotgun and raced outside to catch a glimpse of the assailant stealing away in the moonlight. He fired one shot at the retreating figure but missed, and the culprit made his getaway. Bud hurried back into the house to tend to his father.

The critically wounded Talbott lingered in pain until the afternoon of the next day, dying at about 2:00 p.m. September 19. A coroner's jury convened shortly afterward and heard testimony from Bud Talbott and his mother. Bud claimed that the reason he hadn't tried to organize a search party among his neighbors to pursue the supposed assassin was that it simply did not occur to him to do so. The jury concluded that the victim had been killed by a party or parties unknown, but some people questioned the hasty verdict.

In trying to unravel the circumstances of the murder, investigators placed little stock in the doctor's deathbed declaration. Many people believed, according to a Maryville correspondent to the *Chicago Times*, that Talbott's mind "was not exactly sound on the greenback question. There are numerous theories regarding his death, but the generally received opinion is that some person with whom he has had dealings and a falling out has committed the foul deed. No person believes politics had anything to do with the murder."

In fact, Talbott's bizarre deathbed statement aroused enough doubt that suspicion began to settle on the doctor's own family. Although few people openly asserted that Bud or Ed Talbott had killed his father, there were, according to a St. Joseph newspaperman, "dark suspicions whispered about from man to man, grave nods exchanged by thinking heads, terrible insinuations bandied by incautious lips." Dr. Talbott's dying declaration was considered "a most singular statement to be made by any man, more especially by a man of acknowledgedly hard sense and sound judgment. National banks do not employ assassins. Enemies of the cause of Greenbackism do not seek the extermination of the leaders of that party by the knife and the bullet." Most people thought it impossible that Dr. Talbott actually believed his own statement. And if he knew or suspected the identity of the person who'd fired the deadly shot, why would he not want to cast suspicion on that person?

Other factors also contributed to the widespread skepticism with which Bud Talbott's version of events was greeted. The initial investigation revealed that the window through which the assassin had supposedly fired had not been cleanly pierced as if by a bullet but instead had been broken as if by a stick or a piece of metal and the pieces had fallen outside, not inside as one might expect if the shattering force had come from outside. In addition to Bud's failure to organize a posse, the fact that he and the rest of the Talbott family showed little concern as the doctor lay dying seemed strange as well. Also, Talbott was known for his stinginess and harsh treatment toward his wife and sons, and it was rumored that he had administered a particularly severe beating to Bud just a few days before his murder and that the young man had vowed revenge.

One night just a few days after Dr. Talbott's murder, shots were heard coming from the Talbott residence, and when neighbors came to investigate, the family claimed the house had been attacked by armed men and that the intruders had been repelled only after a heated, close-range gunfight.

Investigators found numerous bullet holes in the walls and ceiling. After this strange occurrence, shots were fired at the Talbott place several nights in a row. The Talbotts reported that someone was out for their blood, but when the sheriff offered to post deputies at the house, the offer was declined.

Most people familiar with the case gradually concluded that Dr. Talbott had "groaned out his life in bitter silence" to protect his family. Detectives were put on the case to obtain additional evidence, and one of them, Jonas V. Brighton, found work under the name of Frank Hudson on a farm neighboring the Talbott place. Brighton and his wife, Virginia, whom he represented as his sister Jennie, moved into a tenant house on the farm and quickly became acquainted with the Talbott brothers. According to later reports, "Miss Hudson" feigned romantic interest in Bud to gain his confidence, and he soon confessed his involvement in his father's murder to the young woman and her "brother."

Brighton, who had served a term in the Kansas State Penitentiary for grand larceny, revealed that his real occupation was robbery. He suggested that the Talbott brothers go into an outlaw partnership with him and Jennie, and they agreed. Wilford Mitchell, Belle Talbott's brother-in-law, got in on the scheme, too, and all five parties signed a contract, dated October 25, 1880, binding them together "for the purpose of bank robbing, train robbing and stage robbing, and safes." The signees swore that they would stay at each other's side until death in any attempt to obtain booty and that they understood that anyone deserting during such an attempt would be killed. After the first successful robbery, any member of the gang could quit if he or she chose to do so, but the person must first equally divide any loot obtained during the robbery and swear under penalty of death not to betray the remaining members.

Brighton promptly relayed the news of Bud Talbott's confession to Nodaway County authorities, and he also turned over the contract he and the other four "bank robbers" had signed. In addition, Brighton reported that the Talbotts had offered him $50 to kill the hired man, Henry Wyatt, because Wyatt was in on the murder of Dr. Talbott and the brothers were afraid he would give them away.

Acting on Brighton's statement and evidence he had gathered himself, Sheriff Henry Toel arrested the Talbott brothers and Henry Wyatt on October 26 and escorted them to the Nodaway County Jail in Maryville. Later the same day, Mrs. Talbott was arrested as an accessory and also taken to Maryville. A preliminary examination began on the 27th before Judge Stephen Morehouse.

At the hearing, Brighton described how he and his wife had inveigled their way into the Talbott boys' confidence and the brothers had revealed their secrets to them. Interviewed by a newspaperman after he left the witness stand, Brighton added that Bud had remarked on Dr. Talbott's meanness and said, with a show of bravado, that he was brought up to do what he did—kill his father. In addition, Ed Talbott had allegedly told Brighton that Henry Wyatt had killed W. R. Saunders, a prominent Maryville citizen who'd been mysteriously murdered some months earlier.

Wilford Mitchell, who was in on Brighton's scheme to trap the Talbott boys, took the stand after Brighton and testified that Bud had told him that he and Henry Wyatt had plotted together to kill Dr. Talbott. Bud had made the ball and loaded the gun but Wyatt had fired the fatal shot while Bud sat in the house in the same room as his father. Wyatt, on the other hand, told Mitchell that Bud had fired the fatal shot.

Mitchell said that Bud told him he and Wyatt had first started plotting to kill his father several months earlier. Mitchell also added that Belle had told him that she and Dr. Talbott did not live together agreeably and that he had abused her.

Next up on the witness stand was Sheriff Toel. He said that, after the suspects had been arrested, Henry Wyatt had requested and was granted a private interview with him.

Wyatt admitted that he knew ahead of time about the plot to kill Dr. Talbott and that the gun had been loaded and kept upstairs for about eight days before the murder. However, Wyatt said that he wasn't even present when the shooting occurred but that the Talbott boys had told him later how it happened. When Dr. Talbott arrived home on the fateful night, Ed went downstairs with the loaded gun, went outside with it, and knelt under the window. Bud came into the room and sat down near the window. He moved the curtain aside to give his brother a clear view, and Ed fired through the window at his father.

Other witnesses confirmed that Dr. Talbott had treated his family with extreme harshness.

At the close of the preliminary hearing, Bud Talbott, Ed Talbott, and Henry Wyatt were held on first degree murder charges, Bud as the principal and the other two as accessories before the fact. All three were committed to jail without bail. Belle Talbott, who was thought to have known about the plot to kill her husband but not to have actively participated in it, was also charged as an accessory. She was held on $1,000 bond.

At the November term of the Nodaway County Circuit Court, the Talbott brothers and Wyatt were formally indicted for the murder of Perry Talbott, and Wyatt's case was severed from that of the Talbott brothers. Bud and Ed pleaded not guilty at arraignment, and their case was continued until January of 1881. The grand jury declined to indict Belle Talbott, and she was released.

When the trial for the Talbott brothers got underway during the third week of January, Jonas Brighton was one of the main witnesses against the defendants. He repeated much the same testimony he'd given at the preliminary hearing, telling how the Talbott boys had offered to pay him $50 to kill Henry Wyatt so that Wyatt wouldn't tell what he knew about the murder of Dr. Talbott. On cross-examination, defense attorney Lafe Dawson tried to impeach Brighton's testimony by attacking his character. Dawson pointed out that the witness had spent time in the Kansas State Penitentiary, and he also claimed that Brighton had married his wife, Virginia, while she was still married to another man.

Virginia Brighton also took the witness stand for the prosecution. She said she'd overheard Bud Talbott tell her husband that he'd pay him $50 for killing Wyatt if Ed didn't. Later Bud boasted to her that it was not a big deal to kill a man and that he would kill Wyatt himself except that he had been into so much meanness that everybody in the neighborhood was watching him. Once again the defense tried to impeach the witness by attacking her character, asking her whether it was not true that she had married Brighton while still legally married to her previous husband and that she'd once been arrested for public indeceny. She refused to answer the first allegation and denied the second.

After Mrs. Brighton stepped down, the courtroom was thrown into excitement when Sheriff Toel walked in with Henry Wyatt and led him to the witness stand. Agreeing to turn state's evidence, Wyatt said he wished to tell all he knew about the murder of Dr. Talbott. He said that the Talbott brothers had first made plans to kill their father about six weeks before he was shot and that several different schemes, which Wyatt himself was in on, had either failed or not been carried through. The boys loaded a gun in an upstairs room a few days before the killing. On the fateful night, Ed, leaving Wyatt upstairs, took the gun downstairs. Wyatt soon heard a shot, and the brothers later told him what happened. Ed fired the shot through the front window, laid the gun down, and ran around the house to the kitchen door, while Bud raced out the front door, picked up the gun, and fired a shot at a make-believe assassin. Wyatt denied that he'd ever told Wilford Mitchell who shot Dr. Talbott. The only person he'd told, he said, was Sheriff Toel.

When it came time for the defense lawyers to present their case, they stuck to their strategy of attacking the state's chief witnesses. Numerous depositions were taken and several witnesses paraded to the stand testifying to the fact that the reputations of both Jonas Brighton and his wife were bad—that Jonas was a thief and Virginia a prostitute. Two witnesses testified that Jonas Brighton had told one of them that, if he (Brighton) could get the Talbott brothers indicted, they would pay him $10,000 to leave the territory. Also, Bud and Ed's fourteen-year-old brother, William, said he'd never seen his father knock either of his older brothers down.

The trial continued throughout the fourth week of January. Friday evening the 28th, the jury came back from deliberations with a verdict declaring the brothers guilty of first degree murder. The next day Judge John C. Howell denied a defense motion for a new trial and pronounced sentence. Addressing each defendant separately, Howell asked whether there was any reason why he should not be sentenced to death, and each in turn said, "Yes, because I'm not guilty." The judge replied that the jury had said otherwise, and he sentenced both young men to be hanged on March 25.

The decree evoked what one newspaper called a "heartrending scene" in the courtroom:

> Women cried and shrieked as if in agony. Strong men wept. The terrible scene of mother, sister and other relatives of the convicted and sentenced boys as they wrapped their arms around their necks and wept as if their hearts would break. Albert broke completely down and wept like a child.

After sentence was pronounced, the Talbott boys were led back to the Nodaway County Jail, where they were visited the next day, Sunday the 30th, by a *Maryville Democrat* reporter. They talked freely, saying they had slept well the night before after the harrowing experience of their trial. They proclaimed their innocence and said they had not given up hope. They spoke of Judge Howell and other officers of the court in favorable terms, and they said they thought they'd gotten a fair trial, except that some of the prosecution witnesses had sworn falsely against them. Asked about a possible commutation of sentence, Bud said he'd rather go ahead and hang on March 25 as scheduled than spend the rest of his life in prison, but Ed differed, pointing out that as long as he was alive there was hope of an escape or a pardon.

Bud need not have worried about hanging on March 25, because his attorneys appealed the verdict to the Missouri Supreme Court, which stayed the execution until mid-May, pending the outcome of the appeal.

On February 2, Bud and Ed Talbott were taken from Maryville to St. Joseph for safekeeping. A St. Joseph newspaperman called at the Buchanan County Jail to interview the prisoners, but they declined to talk, upon the advice of their attorneys. However, the reporter got a good look at them. He described them as being "of medium height, of dark complexion, hair and eyes." Bud had a small, brown mustache, while Ed's smooth face looked as if it was "innocent of a razor." Both boys looked a little haggard and worn but otherwise had a "rather prepossessing" appearance.

After a plot to free the Talbott brothers from the Buchanan County Jail was uncovered in early March, they were transferred to the Andrew County Jail in Savannah.

The Missouri high court took up the Talbott case at its April 1881 term. Among the several exceptions filed by the defense was an objection to the fact that a letter dated before Dr. Talbott's murder and later found in Henry Wyatt's coat proposing to kill the doctor was not admitted as evidence. The lawyers claimed the letter was written by Wilford Mitchell and, therefore, tended to exonerate their clients. The Supreme Court ruled that the letter was properly excluded because there was no evidence as to who had written it. On the last day of April, the high court accordingly affirmed the verdict of the lower court and rescheduled the hanging for June 24.

In early to mid-May, a *Maryville Democrat* reporter traveled to Savannah to get the Talbott boys' reaction to the recent ruling affirming their death sentences. Bud said they were a little surprised by the decision but would bear up even if they had to face the gallows. Changing his tune from what he'd said three months earlier, Bud said he'd prefer a life sentence to hanging because he felt sure the true facts of the case would one day come to light, the guilty parties would be brought to justice, and he and his brother would be released. Claiming he and Ed were victims of a conspiracy, Bud said he knew who had really killed his father but that he was not prepared to reveal the name of the person at that moment.

After the interview, a priest who had been offering spiritual advice to the Talbott brothers told the reporter that the young men had also told him they did not murder their father. They claimed that Wilford Mitchell had hired Henry Wyatt to do the job, which was the same line of argument pursued by the defense at trial.

The Talbotts remained at Savannah for several more weeks before being brought back to Maryville to await their awful fate.

Even before the supreme court handed down its decision, Missouri governor Thomas Crittenden had begun to receive letters asking him to commute the sentence of the Talbott brothers. As their rescheduled date with death neared, the volume of letters pleading for clemency increased, and a number of newspapers joined in the chorus, asking the governor to intervene. The *St. Joseph Herald*, for instance, opined that the lives of the Talbott boys should be spared in consideration of several mitigating circumstances, including the extreme youth of Ed Talbott (who was not yet seventeen years old) and the fact that the key witness against the Talbotts was an accomplice in the crime.

On June 10, the condemned prisoners gained an unlikely advocate when Jonas Brighton wrote to defense attorney Dawson on June 10 admitting that he'd plied the Talbotts with whiskey and other intoxicating liquors to loosen their tongues and that he'd represented himself as a killer and a bank robber to gain their confidence. He allowed that these inducements had probably caused the boys to make statements to him falsely incriminating themselves because they had bragged to him about other murders that he knew they had not committed. Brighton said that he agreed with the defense theory that Mitchell and Wyatt had conspired to kill Dr. Talbott and that he thought he could prove it if given an opportunity and a little time. He said he knew Mitchell had sworn falsely in regard to the Talbott case.

Even Henry Wyatt volunteered or was induced to make a statement. On June 21 he told his attorney, who took the statement down in writing, that he had long been subject to fits and wild imaginings. He said he could no longer be sure whether what he'd testified to at the Talbotts' trial was true or something he'd simply pictured in his mind. He admitted that he had turned against the brothers because he thought they wanted to do harm to him. After Wyatt signed the statement, his attorney immediately forwarded it to Governor Crittenden.

On the same day, June 21, Mrs. Talbott traveled with her sons' attorneys to Jefferson City to make a personal appeal to the governor. Despite the in-person interview and the various other pleas for mercy, Crittenden still declined to interfere.

All preparations for the execution, slated for 1:00 p.m. on June 24, were made, and a large crowd gathered in Maryville that morning to witness it. About 9:00 a.m., the sheriff received a last-minute telegram from Crittenden postponing the hanging until July 22. After the sheriff and Prosecuting Attorney W. W. Ramsey sought and received confirmation of the reprieve, Ramsey went to the corner of the public square about 10:30 a.m. and announced to the gathered throng that the execution had been postponed.

The announcement was received with "a surprising degree of quietude." Many in the crowd murmured their discontent, and some severely criticized the governor. However, there was little loud talk and no threatening demonstrations. Still, many feared that some "among the rougher, unthinking, reckless elements of society" might try to organize a mob later on, and extra guards were stationed at the jail during the remainder of the day and overnight.

The next morning, June 25, the Talbott brothers, who said they were not surprised by the governor's reprieve, were again removed from the Nodaway County Jail and taken to St. Joseph for safekeeping.

On July 5, Ed Talbott signed a sworn statement confessing that he had fired the shot that killed his father. He said he and Henry Wyatt had gone to bed in an upstairs room when Dr. Talbott came home on the fateful night. Ed said he soon heard the sounds of a disturbance and his mother crying for help. He and Wyatt ran downstairs and saw Ed's mother on the floor and his father kicking her. Dr. Talbott called for his pistol, which was sitting on a nearby bureau, but instead of retrieving the pistol, Ed grabbed a shotgun and shot his father in the back.

Bud Talbott, who had been to the barn, came inside immediately after the shot was fired and helped his father into bed, while Henry Wyatt left the room. Realizing his wound was fatal, Dr. Talbott called his family to his bedside and, recounting their troubles, said he wanted to forgive and be forgiven. He told his sons to deny everything and that he wanted the public to think the national banks had hired an assassin to kill him because of his speeches denouncing them.

Ed accused Brighton, Mitchell, and Wyatt of swearing falsely, but he didn't blame Wyatt because he had a weak mind.

Bud Talbott signed a statement saying he had read Ed's statement and that it was true as far as he knew from the time he entered the house. Bud said that he had gone outside and fired the gun at the make-believe assassin at his father's direction as a part of the doctor's scheme to cover up the crime and that he had also knocked the glass out of the window at the doctor's direction. Bud said he'd denied everything and even sworn falsely before the coroner's jury for his brother's sake. He added that he'd even been willing to die alongside Ed if his brother preferred to keep the secret, but now that Ed had confessed he was hereby confirming that part of the confession of which he had knowledge.

Many observers believed the boys' affidavits showed "beyond all question the true state of facts" surrounding Dr. Talbott's murder. The *St. Joseph Weekly Gazette*, for instance, felt that the statements vindicated the newspaper's long-held belief that the brothers were not cold-blooded killers and that the statements strengthened the argument that the boys should be shown leniency. But others thought the confession was a self-serving, phony plea for mercy.

Shortly after the Talbotts' statement, Henry Wyatt also issued a statement affirming in every particular what the brothers had said. The *Gazette* opined that Wyatt's supporting statement showed the folly of those skeptics "who too early caviled as to the genuineness of the confession of the younger Talbott." The paper felt there could no longer be any reasonable doubt that Ed's story of the crime was true.

Governor Crittenden, however, was among those not persuaded. As the Talbotts' July 22 date with death approached, the governor resisted renewed calls for him to grant the brothers clemency. On July 18, Crittenden informed Sheriff Toel that he would not interfere further in the execution, and he instructed the sheriff to proceed with the preparations. He said that if Ed Talbott's confession was true, then his and his brother's previous defense, including their appeals to the supreme court and to the governor, was based on a falsehood; that the boys had ample opportunity to tell the truth before now; and that he was not inclined to grant clemency based on a last-minute appeal that might also be a falsehood. The governor also cited the fact that Mrs. Talbott had not confirmed Ed's confession as strong evidence of its untruth.

On the evening of July 20, just a day and a half before the scheduled hanging, Bud Talbott issued a long, detailed confession retracting what Ed had said two weeks earlier, once again fingering Henry Wyatt as the person who had shot

Dr. Talbott, and naming Mitchell as an accomplice. Bud's latest story turned many people who had believed Ed's confession against the Talbotts and soured the faith of those who'd previously argued for clemency.

On July 21, the Talbotts were brought back to Maryville from St. Joseph. About two o'clock the next afternoon, Bud and Ed Talbott, declaring their innocence to the very last, were escorted to a scaffold that had been erected on a hill just northeast of town. They mounted the steps without hesitation and were soon "launched into the presence of their Creator" before twelve to fifteen thousand gaping spectators who had "flocked in from every direction…to feast their eyes on the revolting spectacle."

The bodies were cut down about 3:00 p.m. and placed in coffins, and they were buried the next day in the family plot next to the father that most people—but not everybody—believed they'd killed. The *St. Joseph Weekly Gazette*, one of the Talbott boys' staunches defenders, allowed that most people were in favor of the execution but were motivated more by a morbid desire to see a hanging than by a sense of justice.

Chapter Six

Midnight Tragedy in Lucas Place
The Murder of Fred Thomkins and the Trial of Kitty Mulcahy

Near midnight on Sunday evening, December 18, 1881, John Powers, night watchman in the exclusive Lucas Place residential district of St. Louis, heard the sound of a gunshot come from near the corner of Seventeenth and Lucas Place (i.e. Locust Street). Rushing to the scene, he found Fred Thomkins (aka Tonkin) lying mortally wounded in a grassy plot just outside the enclosed churchyard of the Second Presbyterian Church with a bullet wound to his gut. The twenty-seven-year-old Thomkins, according to the *St. Louis Post Dispatch*, was known about the neighborhood as a voyeur and "amateur blackmailer" who was in the habit of spying on people who resorted to the churchyard for "immoral purposes" and then extorting those he found in "compromising situations." Powers had warned Thomkins his perverse curiosity was going to get him in trouble, and now it had seemingly gotten him killed.

Thomkins told Powers that he'd followed a young man and a young woman to the churchyard, that they'd caught him watching them, and that the young man had shot him as he and the woman rushed out of the courtyard. The only evidence left behind was a seal-skin cap the woman had dropped.

Thomkins repeated essentially the same story after he was taken to the city hospital, but his version of events contained so many contradictions that authorities placed little stock in what he said. Also, Charles Turner, an eyewitness who lived just across the street from the church, swore that the young woman fired the shot.

Two different women were arrested on Monday as suspects and brought before Thomkins, but he said neither was the woman he'd seen at the churchyard. Thomkins died later that night.

On Tuesday night, a young woman named Kitty Mulcahy, suspecting of firing the fatal shot, was arrested at a bordello on Eighth Street run by Lou Allen. Then, in the wee hours of the morning on Wednesday the 21st, eighteen-year-old Billy Scharlow was rousted out of bed at his mother's home on Biddle Street and taken into custody as Kitty's suspected accomplice.

Interviewed later on Wednesday, Lou Allen told a *Post-Dispatch* reporter that she'd known Kitty ever since she was a child. Kitty had previously been married but was only eighteen and was "a nice sweet-tempered little girl." She had a lover named Billy Scharlow who frequently called on her at Lou's place, and the two had been out together Sunday night. Lou said the girl's real name was McCabe, although she went by several different names, including Mulcahy and Lamont.

After talking to Lou, the reporter went to the jail to see Kitty. The newspaperman thought she was "not a bad looking girl," but her short, tangled hair gave her an appearance that was "not exactly what a fastidious man would demand of his lady love." And Kitty's expletive-laden answers to the reporter's questions suggested she was not at all the sweet-tempered girl Lou had made her out to be.

Angry that Lou had apparently turned her in after she'd confided in her, Kitty called the madam a damned bitch and refused at first to talk about what happened Sunday night. "What the _____ and _____ do you want to know for, you ____ _____ _____?" she swore.

She finally calmed down enough to tell her story, which the reporter related, "stripped of its curses and vulgarity." Kitty admitted that she was near the church on

Sunday night and heard the shot that killed Thomkins. However, she claimed that she was not the person who fired the shot and that Billy was nowhere near the scene. Instead, she tried to implicate "a Kerry Patch dame" (a girl from the Irish neighborhood) named Mollie Maloney, who was her rival for Billy's affections.

The reporter asked Kitty about several elements of her story that he'd learned from Lou Allen, and she "contradicted herself in every particular," denying she'd said those things. Then when she went back over her own version of the story, she "got it tangled worse than ever." The only consistent part of her story was her insistence that Billy had nothing to do with the crime.

A coroner's inquest began Wednesday afternoon, but Kitty did not testify until Thursday morning, when she "came in smiling, dressed in a showy red dress, with a red hood and black cloak. She smiled pleasantly at Billy Scharlow, winked at the reporters, flung herself into a chair, and crossed her legs." Kitty kept her eyes fastened on Billy, but he seemed to ignore her.

When Kitty took the stand, there was a stir of interest among the jury, and all listened intently as the coroner questioned her. She introduced herself as Kitty Lamont but added that she had "half a dozen" other names, one of which was Mulcahy. Kitty repeated essentially the same story she'd told the reporter the day before, admitting that she heard the shot that killed Thomkins but that she didn't fire it and that Billy was nowhere near. She admitted that, shortly before the shooting, a man had offered to give her a seal-skin cap and $2 if she'd go to his room with him, but she said she did not accept the offer. Instead, she once again tried to implicate Mollie Maloney, but the police felt sure that Kitty and Billy were the guilty pair, although they now believed that Billy had fired the fatal shot, as Thomkins had said.

The inquest ended on Friday morning, December 23, and Kitty reportedly grew uneasy when the verdict was not

Sketch of Kitty Mulcahy. *From the St. Louis Post-Dispatch*

announced at once. The longer the announcement was
delayed, the more restless she became. That afternoon,
officers took her back over the route she said she'd walked
on the night of the shooting, having her repeat her story as
she went along, and they found several contradictions in her
new story. Back at the police station, she implicated a man
named Buckley, who had testified at the coroner's inquest,
but confronted by Buckley when he was brought in, she
broke down and said that she had fired the shot that killed
Thomkins. She claimed the man she was with, though, was
not Billy Scharlow but rather a man she'd just met minutes
before the shooting. She didn't know his name because, in
her words, "We never ask anyone who we meet that way
about their name." The stranger she was with had virtually
forced a pistol into her hand when Thomkins appeared and
urged her to shoot the peeping Tom.

A day or two later, a lawyer called on Kitty, and she temporarily recanted her confession on his advice. By Monday, December 26, however, she had reverted to the confession. She told a *Post-Dispatch* reporter that she shot Thomkins because he was coming at her and because she didn't realize how easily the pistol would fire. She said she loved Billy Scharlow and said she planned to marry him if she got out of jail.

"In telling her story, Kitty acted in a very childish way," according to the reporter, and she admitted that her role at Lou Allen's place was to play the "child girl." Although some policemen and other observers believed Kitty's story, many others felt she was just trying to shield Scharlow.

The reporter also talked to Scharlow the same day he interviewed Kitty. Billy said Kitty went by Lamont because that was her married name. She and her husband were separated but not divorced. She often went by Mulcahy but her real maiden name was McKaye. Billy said he didn't know what to make of Kitty's confession, because she hadn't mentioned a word about it to him when he saw her the day after the shooting.

Both Kitty and Billy were released shortly after the reporter talked to them, but Billy was soon returned to custody on a prior assault charge. Then, on December 28, Kitty was charged with murder for the Thomkins killing. Upon her arrest, she said that, since Billy was going to the penitentiary, she didn't care if she did, too. "If he was to go to hell, I would want to go," she declared.

Kitty complained about a sketch of her that had appeared in the *Post-Dispatch* the previous day, saying it didn't look like her at all. "When I was with the May Fiske blondes," she said, "I looked pretty good." (The May Fiske Blondes was a traveling theatrical troupe.)

Kitty's preliminary hearing was scheduled for January 6, 1882, but her lawyer got the case continued until the 25th. Kitty did not even appear in court but "remained in the cage smoking a big cigar." A *Post-Dispatch* reporter also found her childishly climbing up and down the iron bars and remarking to the jailer that she was a monkey. In an interview with the reporter, she recanted her previous confession, saying the detectives had coaxed it out of her by plying her with whiskey and cigars. "I was drunk when I gave that confession," she said.

On the night on January 9, Kitty had to be placed in the "dark cell" because of her "indecorous behavior" at the Four Courts Jail.

On January 18, Bill Scharlow was sentenced to two years in the penitentiary on the assault charge. On January 26, Kitty's trial was continued again. At her arraignment in mid-March, she pleaded not guilty.

In late March, an old pistol was found near the scene of the Thomkins murder. It was thought at first that it might be the murder weapon, and a *Post-Dispatch* reporter called on Kitty at the jail to get her reaction to the new clue. "I don't know whether it is any clue or not," she swore, "and I don't care a damn either." She reiterated that she'd only confessed because the officers had given her whiskey and cigars, and she accused Lou Allen of lying about what Kitty had told her just to get in solid with the police so they wouldn't raid her place.

Jury selection in Kitty's case was completed in the late afternoon of April 10, and testimony had scarcely commenced when court was adjourned for the day. The next morning, Kitty "bounded up the stairway" leading to the courtroom "two or three steps at a time" and "seemed in the most cheerful spirits, as though she had not a care or fear on earth."

Almost from the time Kitty was arrested, many people felt that the case against her was weak, and it fell apart when her attorney, J. G. Boyle, presented the defense on April 12. Boyle argued that her confession had been coerced and cajoled out of her, that the case boiled down to a matter of her word against Lou Allen's, and that Lou's testimony was just hearsay at any rate. Kitty was found not guilty later the same day.

The detective to whom Kitty confessed came under criticism for his failure to make a case against her, but he insisted that she had committed the deed. In addition, a woman who had been a cellmate of Kitty's came forward to say that Kitty had admitted the shooting to her, too. But Kitty remained a free woman, and no one else was ever charged for the crime.

On May 2, 1882, less than a month after she'd been acquitted, Kitty made the news again after she and another young woman had rented a room in the vicinity of Eighth and Olive streets. Neighbors learned "the fact of the now celebrated woman being in their midst" and started "making a tremendous kick." Kitty Mulcahy, the *Post-Dispatch* reported, had once again taken up the "life of an abandoned woman" but "now sails under the more aesthetic name of Kitty Lamont"

The businessmen around Eighth and Olive contacted authorities about the bothersome young women in their midst, and an officer contacted Kitty and asked her to move. Kitty complied "with reluctance."

In early December of 1882, Kitty was arrested and charged with larceny. She caused a scene at her arraignment in the Court of Criminal Correction on December 11 when a deputy called for her to "come out," and "Kitty's squeaky voice was heard in the recesses of the dock answering, 'How the hell kin I, Mister, when you've got me locked up?'"

Kitty had another run-in with the law in July of 1883 when she was arrested on a charge of being drunk on the street after an officer found her lying on the sidewalk in an apparent drunken stupor on the night of the 16th. At her hearing the next day in the Second District Police Court, however, she claimed she was not drunk but instead had been thrown from a spring wagon while out riding with two young men and the rear seat of the wagon became detached. She had to be treated at a dispensary for her injuries, and she displayed two wounds on her head that she had received when she hit the ground. The judge promptly dismissed the case.

In March of 1886, the *Post-Dispatch* did a feature on Kitty Mulcahy, recalling her role as a central figure in the Fred Thomkins murder case a few years earlier and sketching her fall "from the throne back to her home in the gutter." Once known as the "hoodlum queen," she was just "a miserable little drunkard now." This was apparently the last word on Kitty Mulcahy.

Billy Scharlow, though, made headlines again in February 1890 when he escaped from the city work-house He was serving a nine-month sentence at the work-house for petit larceny at the time of his escape, but, according to a *Post-Dispatch* report at the time, Billy had "a bad record" that stretched back ten years. In addition to serving time in the state penitentiary on the assault charge that was hanging over him at the time of the Thomkins case, Billy had also "been up on other charges."

Chapter Seven

Whiskey and Bad Women
The Murder of Tom Howard and the Hanging of William Fox

After Thomas Howard's body was found near the train depot in Nevada, Missouri, Sunday morning, May 20, 1883, twenty-two-year-old William Fox was immediately suspected of the crime because he'd been seen drinking and carousing with the victim the night before. On Monday, Tom Archer, an acquaintance of Fox, claimed Fox had confessed to him that he'd killed Howard in a fight over a woman of ill repute named Jane Rose. Arrested and charged with murder, Fox denied the crime and tried to implicate Archer instead, but a day or two later, the prisoner admitted the murder, giving as his motive an old grudge dating back a couple of years when he and Howard both lived in Audrain County. The "general impression" around Nevada, though, was that Fox had killed Howard for his money, and this was the prosecution's theory of the case at trial in early June. Fox's court-appointed attorneys, E. E. Kimball and D. P. Stratton, insisted, on the other hand, that the real story of the murder was the one Fox originally told Tom Archer, that it was a crime of passion, and that their client should be spared the death penalty.

Kimball and Stratton's argument fell on deaf ears, and Fox was convicted of first-degree murder and hanged in late December of 1883. Shortly afterward, new evidence came out to support the defense's theory that Fox might, indeed, have been "acting the hero" and trying to protect

Mrs. Rose in confessing that he'd killed Howard over an old grudge.

But by then, of course, it was too late to save Bill Fox.

Thomas Howard, about thirty-five, was a peddler of pictures, books, and other miscellaneous items. He had previously lived in north Missouri, selling his wares in Audrain and surrounding counties. He was connected to the Howard family of Calloway County, where two of his kinsmen were prominent physicians, but, according to the *St. Louis Post-Dispatch*, he was "unlike his estimable relatives." Instead, he was "very much addicted to drink and of a very licentious nature." In 1880, he married Arimenta Moore, and the couple took up residence in Audrain County. Two years later, they moved to Vernon County, settling in Moundville. Saturday morning, May 19, 1883, Howard left his wife at home in Moundville while he trekked to Nevada and started on one of his drunken sprees.

William Fox was also from north Missouri, having grown up in Audrain County. He married his cousin Mary Trimble there when he was just eighteen years old, but he and his wife didn't get along and were separated off and on. Much like Tom Howard, Fox started carousing and chasing after lewd women, and he and Howard became occasional drinking buddies.

In the fall of 1882, Fox and his wife moved with his parents, Milton and Delilah Fox, to Vernon County. The father worked a farm outside Nevada, but young Fox soon split with his wife again and started spending most of his time in town. In February 1883, he met Jane "Jennie" Rose at the city hall, where she was answering a charge of keeping a house of ill repute. Although Jennie was married and had a reputation as "a common prostitute," Fox became enamored with her and started spending time with her. In early May, the two took a trip together to Hannibal, Missouri, and upon their return to Nevada, Fox started boarding with Jennie and her husband.

Tom Howard and Bill Fox got together in Nevada in the early evening of May 19 and, after renewing their acquaintance, started hitting the saloons. They were last seen about 10 p.m. leaving one of the dives together.

A train derailment occurred in Nevada on the early morning of the May 20, and a stream of curious residents went out to the tracks to gaze at the wreck. About eleven a.m., two young men among the onlookers stumbled upon a man's body south of the depot near "The Cave," a notorious hangout for dissolute men and women. The young men at once notified authorities, who repaired to the scene and determined, from the condition of the body, that the man had been dead only a matter of hours. A piece of paper was found inside one of the man's pockets with "W. T. Howard, Moundville, Mo." written on it. The county coroner called an inquest, and an acquaintance of Thomas Howard confirmed the dead man's identity.

Howard's body was then taken to the Nevada City Hall, where the inquest resumed. The examiners found a bullet had passed through one of Howard's ears, another had grazed his cheek, and two were lodged in his body.

Having been seen with Howard the previous day, Fox was one of the people interviewed by the coroner's jury Sunday night. He admitted he'd been with Howard on Saturday evening, but he claimed that they'd parted about 10 p.m., just after leaving one of the downtown saloons, and that he had not seen Howard since.

The jury continued to grill Fox the next day. He had spent over $10 on a pair of boots and a pair of pants on Sunday morning, and the investigators, suspecting that Fox might have killed Howard for the money he was known to have been carrying Saturday evening, wanted the witness to explain where he got the money to buy the goods. Fox said he had $40 when he came back from Hannibal with Mrs. Rose and that she'd been keeping the money for him. He said he thought Tom Archer had killed Howard in a dispute over Lou Higgins, another married prostitute. The jurors found so many inconsistencies in Fox's testimony, however, that he remained a prime suspect in the case, and both he and Arnold were arrested Monday evening on suspicion.

Interrogated at the city jail, Archer said he'd met Fox near the Cave early Sunday morning and that Fox confessed he'd killed Howard the night before. According to Archer's story of what Fox said, Howard wanted Fox to fix him up with a prostitute, and Fox had introduced Howard to Jennie Rose in the woods near the Cave. Howard argued with Jennie over payment, and Fox killed Howard when he started roughing the woman up. Offering a motive for why Fox had turned against him and accused him of the crime, Archer said he'd told Fox after the coroner's jury adjourned on Sunday night that he would have no more to do with trying to cover up the crime. Archer added that he had not come forward sooner because he was afraid a mob would lynch both him and Fox before he had a chance to prove his innocence.

Mrs. Rose was arrested Tuesday morning but was released with the understanding that she would return later in the day to give a full statement of everything she knew about the case. That afternoon she told authorities she had no connection to the murder whatsoever except that Fox had come to her Sunday evening and confessed the deed. According to Jennie's story, Fox told her he'd already confessed to Archer but he didn't think Archer would say anything. If Archer did talk, Fox said he would implicate Archer in the crime. Fox then threatened to kill Mrs. Rose if she told what she knew or refused to provide him an alibi about where his money came from.

After Jennie's testimony, both she and Archer were released, and the next day, Wednesday the 23rd, Fox gave a written confession exonerating both of them. It was considerably different from the story he'd told Archer. Fox said that, after hitting the saloons with Howard, he suggested they go to the Cave and "see the girls." Howard agreed, and they started in that direction. By the time they neared the

Cave, Fox had made up his mind to kill Howard to avenge an old grudge.

Back when Fox had lived in Audrain County, he'd left the county shortly after a farmer's hog went missing, and some people suspected him of the theft. Upon his return to Audrain, Howard said to him in front of a saloon full of men that it "looked suspicious" for him to leave the area while under accusations of stealing. An angry argument ensued, and Fox vowed to get even with Howard for the public insult. The two men had not spoken to each other since the incident until Howard approached Fox in Nevada in a friendly manner as if nothing had happened. Fox, though, had not forgotten the slight, and now he meant to have his revenge.

As Fox and Howard passed through the woods near the cave, Fox sat down on a rock as though to rest. When Howard walked on a few more steps, Fox drew his revolver and shot him in the back. After the first shot, Howard slumped to the ground but was able to turn to Fox and beg him not to shoot again. Fox coolly shot the fallen man a second time, and he collapsed, mortally wounded. Fox said he then fired one more shot at Howard's head but could not account for the supposed fourth shot.

Howard died within a couple of minutes after the final shot. Fox then rifled through his pockets, taking $40 in cash and a few other items. After hanging around the crime scene about half an hour contemplating his next move, Fox went to Jennie Rose's house and told her what he'd done. Concluding his confession, Fox asserted positively that neither Archer nor Mrs. Rose knew anything about the killing until after the fact, but his admission that he went to Jennie's house almost immediately after the killing contradicted her statement that she first learned of the murder on Sunday evening.

Based on Fox's confession, a special grand jury of the Vernon County Circuit Court indicted him for first degree murder on May 24. Appearing for arraignment the next day, he pleaded guilty, but Judge Charles Burton refused to accept the plea and appointed lawyers Kimball and Stratton to defend him.

The attorneys requested and were granted a continuance until June 6 so that they could prepare for trial. On the eve of the trial, a *Nevada Democrat* reporter interviewed Fox at the Vernon County Jail. The prisoner freely admitted his crime, he said he didn't want others to suffer on his account, and he expressed a wish to be speedily hanged. He added that he preferred "stretching hemp" to imprisonment in the state penitentiary at Jefferson City, but he was afraid his lawyers might be "too talented" and would make an effort to "save his neck from the halter."

His attorneys did make an effort, but they only succeeded in postponing Fox's fate.

When trial began on the 6th, the prosecution, reflecting the general feeling around Nevada, argued that Fox had killed Howard strictly for his money. Even if Fox's elaborate explanation for the murder was true, it meant that he had killed his victim over a trivial grudge. In either case, he was guilty of first degree murder.

Fox's lawyers, on the other hand, argued that there were mitigating factors. They said Fox loved Mrs. Rose, even though she was a dissolute woman, and that their client's original story to Arnold that he'd killed Howard because Howard had struck or tried to strike Mrs. Rose was the true story. Fox had only changed his story to protect her from involvement in the crime, and he had acted out of passion, not out of greed or revenge as the other theories of the crime held. The defense further held that Fox was not fully sane and, therefore, not responsible for his actions.

The presentation of evidence lasted throughout the day, and the jury retired to deliberate on the night of the 6th. The next morning, June 7, they announced a verdict of guilty. Fox's lawyers immediately asked for a new trial, but the judge overruled the motion and sentenced Fox to hang on July 18, 1883.

The case was then appealed to the Missouri Supreme Court, which issued a stay of execution to give time for the appeal to be considered. The high court took up the case in October. The defense based its appeal partly on the fact that someone had tossed a hangman's noose into the jury room during deliberations, causing the jury to be unduly prejudiced against Fox. The high court rejected the argument, because the judge had offered the defense an opportunity to question the jurors as to any prejudicial effect the noose might have had and the lawyers had declined. The appellants also argued that they should have been granted a longer continuance to give them time to gather depositions in Audrain County testifying to Fox's insanity. The Supreme Court rejected this argument as well, pointing out that the deponents had been ready to give their statements on June 4, two days before Fox's trial began, but that the defense lawyers declined to take the statements on that date, even though they were present in Audrain County. In addition, Kimball and Stratton had announced their readiness for trial before the proceeding began on June 6. The verdict was, therefore, affirmed and Fox's execution reset for December 28.

When a *Sedalia Bazoo* newspaperman called on Fox in his cell on December 9, the prisoner told the reporter that he had professed religion, was regularly visited by ministers, and planned to be baptized. His wife, Mary, also visited him frequently, and, according to the reporter, seemed very devoted to him in spite of everything he had done. Although he'd given a detailed confession six months earlier, he now refused to say why he had killed Howard.

On Sunday, December 16th, Fox was taken in handcuffs to the local Christian Church and baptized. Back at the jail the next day, he refused to enter his cell and seemed determined to make Sheriff William Fisher have to shoot him but finally went into the cell of his own accord. The sheriff noted that this was the only time Fox had ever given him trouble.

On December 27, the day before the scheduled execution, Fox was again interviewed in his cell at the Nevada jail. He blamed his downfall on "whiskey and bad women." In addition, he said that he had gotten married too young and married a woman to whom he was "too closely related." He and his wife were too much alike and, therefore, couldn't get along. The main reason he offered for his wayward life and for the murder of Howard, however, was simply, "Something has been always wrong with my head."

When the reporter first broached the subject of Howard's murder, Fox said he didn't want to talk about it, but when the newspaperman persisted, the prisoner grudgingly answered a few questions. Asked whether he had told the truth in his written confession, Fox said he had not. He said he was desperate and despairing at the time and had told a story he thought would get him hanged as quickly as possible.

Pressed on Mrs. Rose's possible involvement in or preknowledge of the crime, Fox refused to answer. Asked specifically whether she was present at the time of the killing, Fox again would not say.

Perhaps Fox was trying to protect Jennie, but the evasiveness of his answers soon began to implicate her instead.

Asked whether he took a pistol and knife off Howard's body, Fox answered, "Yes, they were ta…." Stopping in mid-sentence to correct himself, he finished, "Yes, I took them."

Asked whether Mrs. Rose had on a hat when he arrived at her house shortly after the murder, he replied, "Not after we got into the house."

Did he split the money with Mrs. Rose, the reporter asked. "I won't say," came the answer.

Whether Fox's slip-ups were unwitting blunders or deliberate revelations calculated to implicate someone else in the crime and mitigate his own guilt is even harder for us to determine from a distance of 135 years than it was for the

Nevada reporter. For an hour, the newspaperman continued to grill the prisoner in an attempt to discover what part, if any, Mrs. Rose played in the crime, but "every approach to the subject was met with a monotonous 'I won't say.'"

Like the reporter, we can only reach one of two conclusions. Either Jennie was indeed involved in the crime and Fox was stubbornly, albeit clumsily, trying to protect her, or else he killed Howard strictly for money and was trying to disguise the fact by hinting that Jennie had some connection to the murder.

Fox declared that he still loved Jennie but that she had treated him very badly since his arrest. He had written to her a number of times, but she had not responded nor been to visit him.

Mrs. Rose's inattention to Fox since his arrest, said the reporter, was the one strong evidence in her favor.

Maybe.

Or maybe not.

Maybe Jennie was just a little smarter and more calculating than her love-struck admirer. One thing about Bill Fox that all reports seemed to agree on was that he was uneducated and dull-witted. It seems almost incredible that he could be shrewd and articulate enough to implicate another person in the murder through manufactured lapses in speech.

Near the end of the interview, Fox asked the reporter about the scaffold and the size of the crowd expected to witness the execution. The prisoner seemed "extremely anxious about making a successful debut on the scaffold."

As the reporter prepared to leave, Fox reiterated that he would go to his grave without revealing the exact manner of the killing.

The next morning, December 28, Milton Fox called at the jail to bid his doomed son a final goodbye, and an hour later Bill Fox's longsuffering wife paid a similar visit. The procession to the gallows, which had been erected on the outskirts of town near the scene of the murder, began shortly after 11:00 a.m.

GONE TO GLORY,

Is the Opinion Entertained by Bill Fox, Who Was Hung Yesterday.

The Brutal Murderer of Tom Howard Swung Into Eternity.

Headline from *Sedalia Weekly Bazoo* describing Fox's hanging.

People had poured into Nevada from all directions, and about 15,000 were gathered on the grounds surrounding the gallows when the carriage Fox was riding in reached the scene. The execution, according to the *Sedalia Weekly Bazoo*, went off very smoothly and without "the usual painful preliminaries." Fox walked firmly up the steps to his doom and went immediately to the trap. At Fox's request, there was no clergy present, and the condemned man gave no lengthy speech, looking out over the crowd and saying only, "Farewell, boys," before the cap was placed over his head and he was swung into eternity at high noon.

After Fox was pronounced dead, the body was cut down, placed in a coffin, and turned over to his father for burial in the family plot.

But that was not quite the end of the story.

Shortly after the execution, Sheriff Fisher revealed that, while riding to the scaffold with Fox, he had tried to get the condemned man to tell the whole truth surrounding the murder if he had not yet done so. As they neared the gallows, the lawman asked Fox whether he had ever told anyone the full story. Fox said the only people who knew all the particulars were two fellow prisoners to whom he had confessed everything, and he gave their names.

On the morning of December 31, a reporter for the Ne*vada Mail* called at the jail to interview the two men. One of the men, J. M. Lundy, had been a jail mate of Fox for several months, and they'd shared the same cell and bunk bed most of that time. Lundy said he and Fox grew to be on very friendly terms during their shared incarceration.

The story Lundy told of the crime, as related to him by Fox, closely matched the tale Fox had told Tom Archer the day after the murder, except that it provided more details. Fox and Howard were headed to Mrs. Rose's after Howard asked his companion to introduce him to some fast women. When they got close, Fox told Howard to wait a short distance away while he (Fox) went inside to make sure Jennie was home. Fox had left a pistol with Jennie, and while in the house, he retrieved it because he'd heard Howard bragging about his pistol and was afraid there might be trouble. Fox and Mrs. Rose had been plotting to run away together, but he asked Jennie not to say anything to Howard about it because Howard knew the Fox family and would tell his wife or parents.

When Howard grew tired of waiting and came to the door, Jennie quickly finished getting ready, and the three started through the woods together. When they got close to the cave, Fox stopped and told Howard and Jennie to go on. He would wait there until they were finished with their business and ready to go home.

Howard and Jennie went on to the cave, and all was quiet for a while. After a few minutes, though, Fox heard the sounds of an argument coming from the cave. He heard Howard yell, "I'll mash your damn mouth!" At first, Fox hesitated, but seconds later he heard Howard's voice again:

"I'll mash your damn face off!" Hearing this, Fox ran to the cave and found Howard and Jennie on the ground with Howard choking her.

Howard wouldn't pay her, Jennie explained as he loosened his grip on her throat.

"That's no way to treat a woman," Fox said. "Let her alone."

"You want to take it up, do you?" Howard said.

"No, I don't want to take it up," Fox said, "but I don't think that's the way to treat a woman."

"You're a damn liar!" Howard exclaimed. "You do want to take it up."

At this challenge, Fox's anger flared. Remembering the old grudge from Audrain County, he drew his pistol and fired two shots at Howard's face. Howard jumped up, turned, and started to run, but Fox stalked after him and shot him twice more, once in the back and once in the side. Howard collapsed and died almost instantly.

After the shooting, Jennie took Howard's money and other possessions off his body, saying she had to be paid something for her trip out here. She kept the money and a few other items but tossed Howard's pistol and knife into the woods.

For some time after the killing, Fox and Jennie stayed in the woods discussing what they should do next. They finally just went back to Mrs. Rose's house and went to bed.

Lundy said Fox had told him the story several times and he always told it the same way. Fox's other jail mate, a man named Gee, confirmed that Fox had told him the same story except that he did not tell Gee the name of the woman involved.

So, was Jennie Rose involved in the murder of Thomas Howard or not? If so, she never paid for her part in the crime. All we know for sure is that Fox had "an unholy and unaccountable attachment" to the woman, as the judge observed in sentencing him to death.

Chapter Eight

Do You Think It Safe to Kill Them?
The Murder of the Sewells and the Hanging of Henry Stair

Around the first of July 1885, Henry S. Stair and Nanetta Osborn came to Nevada, Missouri, from Fort Scott, Kansas. Representing themselves as man and wife, the couple moved into the same house where William Fox had lived at the time he murdered Thomas Howard, and they started running a laundry out of the residence. Shortly afterwards, Jacob Sewell and his fifteen-year-old son, Mack, also came from Fort Scott to Nevada and camped at the edge of town near the fairgrounds. The thirty-four-year-old Stair and the sixty-two-year-old Sewell had met each other over ten years earlier, and the two men renewed their acquaintance. It proved to be an ill-fated reunion for both parties concerned.

A native of Tennessee, Jacob Sewell had come to Missouri as a young man in the early 1850s and settled in northwest Greene County. He and his wife, Evaline, had several children, most of whom grew to adulthood in Greene County. In 1881, their oldest son, John, was killed in Ash Grove when he got into a row with three rowdy Tucker brothers. After Evaline died and the older children were gone from home, Jacob took his youngest son, McClure "Mack" Sewell, and went to Galena, Kansas, where a lead mining boom was going on. He later moved to Fort Scott before coming to Nevada in the summer of 1885.

Henry Stair had seen his share of troubles, too, although some of them were arguably of his own making. He was subject to epileptic seizures when he was growing up in Marshall County, Indiana, according to his father's later testimony, and his parents had to watch him closely to keep him from hurting himself or someone else. Both his family and his neighbors considered him insane, or nearly so. When he was about nineteen, he ran away to New York, but his father, Frederick Stair, traced him there and brought him back home. Rather than place him in an insane asylum, the family once again kept him under a close watch. In 1877, Henry met and married a young woman named Etta Bishop, who proposed to cure him by travel. The couple went to Minnesota, but instead of helping him, the move seemed to make him more unstable to the point that authorities had to place him in an asylum because of his increasingly violent tendencies. Etta came back to Indiana, and about a year later Frederick Stair was able to secure his son's release and bring him back to Indiana as well, although the couple remained estranged. Fred Stair took his son to Arkansas in the fall of 1884 to work in a mill he owned there, but Henry promptly stole $400 from his father and took off. The next thing the father knew about his son was when he heard he was in trouble in Vernon County, Missouri.

The old man's story does not quite jibe, though, with other known facts. According to Fred Stair, for instance, his son got married in the early 1880s to a widow. However, the only known marriage record for Henry S. Stair shows that he married Etta in 1877 and there's no evidence she was married previously. It's possible, of course, that Henry was married more than once, but Fred Stair's recollection of his son's marriage is not the only discrepancy in his story. According to various sources, Henry Stair served a sentence in the Indiana State Penitentiary for forgery and disappeared right after he was released, but the father made no mention of any incarceration other than Henry's stay in the asylum.

In any case, Henry Stair had a checkered past, and he was about to add to his dubious record. In Arkansas, he hooked up with twenty-six-year-old Nanetta Osborn, who was also an Indiana native. The couple came to Fort Scott and then to Nevada, where it didn't take long for Stair to get in trouble again, drawing Nanetta into the scheme with him.

Shortly after Stair and Sewell renewed their acquaintance in Nevada, Sewell took sick, and Stair, accompanied by Nanetta, visited the Sewell camp several times in late July and early August to attend to the patient. At the same time, though, Stair started plotting to steal the old man's horses and other possessions.

On the evening of August 5, Stair and his "wife" went out to the Sewell camp on the north edge of Nevada as they'd been wont to do in recent days. Then, after escorting Nanetta back home about 9:00 or 10:00 p.m., Stair returned to the camp near midnight and killed both Sewell and his son. From later evidence, it was determined that the father was likely killed as he slept in his covered wagon and the son as he slumbered on the ground nearby.

After the murders, Stair loaded the boy's body into the wagon with the father, covered them up with some bedclothes, and then went back home to get Nanetta. The pair returned to the crime scene and hitched up the covered wagon containing the bodies as well as a second wagon of Sewell's. They gathered a few of Sewell's possessions that were scattered about the campground and then started back to Nevada in both wagons. Stair drove the covered wagon with its gruesome cargo, while Nanetta drove the other one.

After retrieving some of their own belongings in Nevada, Stair and Nanetta struck out once again, heading north in the wee hours of the morning on August 6. Stair had planned to dump the bodies at a preselected spot on the Marmaton River, but by the time he and Nanetta reached the river, dawn was breaking and some prospectors were already at work near the spot. The couple were forced to bide their time throughout the daylight hours of the 6th.

Sketch of Henry Stair from *St. Louis Post-Dispatch.*

They camped at first near the prospectors but later moved about a half mile west of the river. That night, Stair dragged the two bodies to the edge of a nearby bluff, placed them beneath an overhang, and covered them with dry leaves and an old gunny sack. He and Nanetta then struck out once again in both wagons, heading east.

Early the next morning, August 7, some people who lived along the river where Stair and Nanetta had tarried the day before and who had become suspicious of the couple decided to investigate. Venturing into the timber, they discovered the dead bodies just hours after they'd been dumped.

Officers were notified, and the desperate duo were overtaken about fifteen miles east of the Marmaton near Harwood. Nanetta was alone in camp when the lawmen arrived, and she reportedly exclaimed as they approached, "Oh, what do you want? What have we done? What have we done?"

Stair, who'd been grazing the horses, soon returned to camp and was placed under arrest, along with Nanetta. In Sewell's covered wagon, the officers found bloody articles of clothing and bedding. Among some papers taken from Sewell's coat pocket they also found a note that read as follows: "Do you think it safe to try to kill them and Rap them up in Cloths, and tell that they went off in Buggy." In light of the overwhelming circumstantial evidence, the two suspects were brought back to Nevada and placed in the Vernon County Jail on the evening of the 7th.

The next night, Saturday, August 8, Nanetta made a confession after Doctor C. A. Rockwood, who was treating her for an illness, told her that a mob was likely forming to lynch Stair but that they would have mercy on her as a woman if she told the full truth. She then implicated Stair in the murders but maintained that she knew nothing about the crime until she discovered one of the bodies in the back of the covered wagon after she and Stair reached the Marmaton River. She said Stair then confessed to her that he and another man had committed the murders, using a knife and a hatchet. A small ax that had been found in one of the wagons was shown to her, but she said it was not the murder weapon. She insisted that a hatchet, not an ax, had been used and that she had not seen the hatchet since she and Stair left the Marmaton.

Evidence that seemed partially to confirm Nanetta's story soon turned up. A knife with blood on it was found in one of the wagons, and a bloody hatchet was found near the place where she and Stair had first camped upon reaching the Marmaton. Since the death wounds were consistent with having been made by such instruments, they were presumed to be the murder weapons Nanetta had mentioned in her confession.

Charged with first degree murder, Henry Stair and Nanetta Osborn waived a preliminary hearing, and their trial was set for late August. E. C. Martindale, prosecuting attorney of Marshall County, Indiana, and a brother-in-law of Stair, traveled to Missouri to represent the defendants.

A grand jury indicted Stair and Osborn on the 22nd, jury selection began on the 26th, and testimony got underway two days later. One of the main prosecution witnesses was Dr. Rockwood, who testified that he was familiar enough with Henry Stair's handwriting that he thought he could recognize it. Handed the note that was found in Stair's coat pocket, Rockwell said that, although he was not positive, he was pretty sure it was Stair's handwriting.

Testifying in his own defense, Stair said he was a victim of circumstances. He claimed he paid Sewell $350 for his teams, that a man named Green was present when he gave Sewell the money, and that Green must have killed Sewell for the money. The defendant said he did not even realize the bodies were in the wagon until he reached the Marmaton. When he discovered them, he grew frightened and disposed of them because he knew appearances were against him.

No one believed Stair's incredible tale, in part because no one believed he ever had anywhere near $350, since he and Nanetta had been living in squalor. Based on the incriminating note and the mountain other circumstantial evidence, the jury came back with a guilty verdict on the evening of September 1 after deliberating only a few minutes. The following morning Judge Charles G. Burton pronounced a sentence of death by hanging for both Stair and Osborn and set the execution date for October 23, 1885.

Martindale promptly appealed the verdict to the Missouri Supreme Court, and the execution was stayed, pending the outcome of the appeal. The high court took up the case without undue delay and handed down a ruling on November 30, 1885. Although Stair and Osborn were jointly indicted and tried, they were arraigned and sentenced separately. The justices held, therefore, that the judgment of the lower court could be affirmed as to one defendant and reversed as to the other, and that's what they did.

Nanetta had denied her guilt from the beginning, claiming that she did not know about the murders until after the fact. The prosecution had used the incriminating note found in Stair's pocket to undermine her statement, suggesting that the note was obviously written to her. The high court disagreed with the prosecution's argument. It might be surmised that the note in question was written and handed to Nanetta Osborn shortly before the murders, but surmises were not sufficient for conviction of first degree murder. The note could have been written at any time, and there was no evidence that Nanetta had any knowledge whatsoever of the note.

The verdict against Stair was, therefore, affirmed, and the verdict against Nanetta Osborn reversed. Stair's execution date was reset for January 15, 1886.

Frederick Stair traveled from Indiana to Missouri in late December 1885 to visit his son, arriving in Nevada on Christmas night. In addition to visiting his son, the father planned, while he was in Missouri, to petition Governor John S. Marmaduke to intercede on behalf of young Stair by issuing either a pardon or a commutation of sentence.

Most observers felt the governor would probably not intervene, and they proved to be right. On January 6, 1886, Marmaduke passed through Nevada on his way back to Jefferson City from Carthage, and he stopped to inquire into the Stair case. Requesting that his identity be kept secret from the prisoner, the governor paid Stair a visit at the Vernon County Jail. After the brief interview, Marmaduke declined to say whether he'd reached a decision in the case, but reporters soon learned that, as he was leaving, he told the sheriff to go ahead with preparations for the execution. The governor made his decision official on January 12, announcing that he would let the law take its course.

On the evening of January 14, the night before Stair was scheduled to hang, his father visited him at 9:00 p.m. and stayed for two hours, after which Stair stayed up writing until about 4:00 o'clock in the morning. He then slept for a little over four hours before awaking to meet his doom shortly after 8:00 a.m. on the 15th.

People flocked into Nevada to witness the hanging, filling all the town's hotels to overflowing on the night of the 14th, and they continued pouring in the next day, with two passenger trains, loaded to capacity, arriving from Kansas City and Sedalia respectively about mid-morning on the 15th. All told, the crowd of curious onlookers surging through the streets of Nevada and gathering at the execution site on the town's eastern edge about a mile from the jail was estimated at 10,000 people.

Fred Stair visited his son again on the morning of January 15 to bid him a final farewell. Then, just after the father took his leave, two ministers arrived about 10:30 a.m. to offer the condemned man spiritual solace. An hour later, Vernon County prosecuting attorney Horace H. Blanton read the death warrant, and then a blacksmith was called to cut the iron bands with which Stair's arms and legs had been bound.

Henry Stair then dressed to meet his doom in a new black suit, white shirt, and black silk tie. He was allowed to visit briefly with Nanetta, but according to at least one report, "The meeting and parting was not of a striking character."

The journey from the jail to the scaffold began about 12:15 p.m. Stair and his escort arrived at the gallows and mounted the scaffold at 12:40. Asked if he had anything to say, the condemned man pulled out a manuscript and read from it, launching into a thirty-minute spiel in which he repeated his claim that he was a victim of circumstances and that he thought Green was the real murderer. Stair also accused Prosecutor Blanton and Sheriff William W. Hill of improper intimacy with Nanetta.

After Stair's lengthy, rambling speech, one of his spiritual advisors offered a prayer and invited those present to join him in singing "Jesus Lover of My Soul." The prisoner joined in. Stair then made a final statement, proclaiming that Nanetta was "as innocent as any lady walking the streets of Nevada" and asking a blessing on his parents and his wife back in Indiana.

Nanetta's sister, Mattie Mulkey, was among the spectators, and Stair tossed a handkerchief to her, asking that it be given to Nanetta. The words written on the handkerchief were dim, but according to one source, Stair declared his love for Nanetta in the message and admitted that he alone had done the killings.

Stair refused to shake hands with Sheriff Hill and Prosecutor Blanton, but he exchanged handshakes with all the others on the scaffold with him. The final preparations for the hanging were then made.

It was 12:28 p.m. when the trap was sprung and Stair shot through the opening to his death. His neck was broken by the fall, and there was no sign of life within a few seconds. The body was cut down after several minutes, placed in a coffin, and later turned over the Fred Stair, who had stayed in his hotel room rather than witness his son's execution. The father took the body home to Indiana for burial.

Nanetta seemed penitent for a while after Stair's execution, according to the 1887 *History of Vernon County*, and she admitted that Stair had committed the murders, while still insisting that she knew nothing about them until after the fact. Her cooperation and seeming contrition evoked a certain amount of sympathy from county officials. Although she soon reverted to her "reckless and depraved" personality, according to the county history, the prosecutor agreed to a plea bargain, and when Nanetta's retrial came up during the May 1886 term of the Vernon County Circuit Court, she pleaded guilty to second-degree manslaughter and received a sentence of five years in the state penitentiary.

In early June, Sheriff Hill escorted her to the Jefferson City prison, and, when her train stopped in Sedalia, a crowd of curious spectators gathered at the depot. A local newspaperman reported, "Mrs. Stair is a coarse looking woman, and was laughing and joking in the most flippant manner with all who came into the car to catch a glimpse of the somewhat noted criminal." When the reporter questioned Nanetta about her seemingly glib attitude, she replied that, although she had been wrongly convicted, she was just trying to be cheerful about the whole thing. She then accepted a cigar that was offered to her and nonchalantly took a puff.

Nanetta was admitted to the state penitentiary under the name Nanetta Stair on June 11, 1886. She was discharged in March 1890 under the state's three-fourths law, which allowed for early release for good behavior. What happened to her after her discharge has not been determined.

Chapter Nine

The Little Chloroformer and the St. Louis Trunk Tragedy

After a man's body was found on the morning of April 14, 1885, stuffed inside a trunk that had been left in Room 144 at the Southern Hotel in St. Louis, detective chief John Burke conducted an initial investigation and announced that he thought the dead man was Charles Arthur Preller, a well-to-do Englishman who had registered at the hotel on April 3. Burke said he thought Preller had been killed by the man assigned to Room 144, another Englishman who had registered at the hotel on March 31 as Walter H. Lennox-Maxwell, M.D.

The murder was baffling because Preller and Lennox-Maxwell had seemed to be intimate friends during their stay at the hotel. The inscription "Thus perish all traitors to the great cause" had been written inside the trunk, and the shape of a cross had been cut on the victim's chest. However, Burke thought this evidence might have been staged to make investigators falsely believe the crime was a political assassination. An empty bottle of chloroform found nearby was thought to be an actual clue, because the dead body showed signs of poisoning. The body was naked except for a pair of undershorts with the name "H. M. Brooks" printed on them. Casual observers speculated at first that the murder scene was a mere hoax perpetrated by medical students, but Burke dismissed such an idea as absurd. "It is a foul murder and nothing less," he told a *St. Louis Post-Dispatch* reporter.

But he could offer no motive for the murder other than the possibility that the victim had been killed for his money.

The reporter concluded that any theory "except that a frightful murder has been committed" was premature. The questions for the police to answer are: Who did the killing? Who was killed? And why was it done?"

As it turned out, Detective Burke had already worked out the answers. Except that greed might not have been the only motive.

Charles Arthur Preller and Hugh Mottram Brooks, traveling under the name Walter H. Lennox-Maxwell, M.D., had sailed from England together in late January aboard the steamship *Cephalonia* and had become fast friends during the journey. The twenty-seven-year-old Preller was a successful traveling salesman for a London textile company, while twenty-four-year-old Lennox-Maxwell was a lawyer who had also studied medicine. The two made plans to travel to Auckland, New Zealand, together, but Preller had business calls to make in North America first. They landed in Boston in early February, and Lennox-Maxwell stayed there while Preller traveled to Canada.

The two agreed to meet in St. Louis, and Lennox-Maxwell arrived there and checked into the Southern Hotel on March 31. He wired Preller, who promptly started for St. Louis, arriving on April 3. Preller was assigned to Room 385, but he spent much of his time in Lennox-Maxwell's Room 144. In the immediate wake of the murder, investigators learned that the hotel staff considered Lennox-Maxwell and Preller good friends and that the two men were "much remarked about the hotel for their dudish, dandified airs."

They came into the dining-room for meals "in a mincing, dancing way," said a hotel clerk, and "neither of them could pass a looking glass in the dining hall without looking in it to see that his mustache was in curl and his hair properly banged."

According to another hotel employee, Lennox-Maxwell, in particular, was considered "a dude from the sole of his foot to the crown of his head.... In his manners he was very effeminate, which he even carried so far as to walk with short, mincing steps like a woman." A letter, deemed "not fit for publication," was later found suggesting a "peculiar" relationship between the two men, although most of the correspondence between them was "just such letters as one friend would write to another."

Hugh M. Brooks and his victim Arthur Preller. *From the St. Louis Post-Dispatch.*

All clues seemed to confirm Detective Burke's initial speculation that the dead man was Preller and that Lennox-Maxwell was the murderer. A small man fitting Lennox-Maxwell's description had twice purchased chloroform from a nearby drugstore on Sunday, April 5, and that night Maxwell had come to the hotel dining room alone, displaying a pistol, boasting about his world travels, and asking odd questions such as how much it would cost in America to hire a lawyer to beat a murder rap. The next morning, Monday, April 6, Lennox-Maxwell spent money extravagantly despite the fact that he'd previously said he was low on funds. Among his purchases were two luggage chests that were delivered to his room at the Southern Hotel, and he also had his beard shaved at a nearby barbershop, where he seemed nervous and in a hurry. Later the same morning, a porter helped him load one of the new chests, now heavy with clothes and other personal belongings, into a carriage outside the hotel, and Lennox-Maxwell left for the train station without checking out of the hotel. At the station, he purchased a ticket for San Francisco and left on a westbound train.

It was concluded that Lennox-Maxwell had taken his belongings out of a large zinc-covered trunk he'd brought from Boston and placed them in the new trunks, then used the old trunk to stash Preller's body on the late afternoon of April 5. The body was not discovered until nine days later, on the morning of April 14, when hotel employees were attracted by a putrid smell emanating from the trunk.

By April 15, the day after the body was discovered, lawmen were virtually certain that Preller was the victim and Lennox-Maxwell the murderer, and they concluded with some certainly as well that the dead man had been poisoned with chloroform. On the same day, confirmation reached St. Louis that a man fitting Lennox-Maxwell's description in almost every detail had arrived in San Francisco on Saturday, April 11. When the ticket he'd purchased in St. Louis was taken up at the San Francisco depot, it bore the name Hugh M. Brooks, the same name inscribed on the dead man's underwear. Subsequent investigation revealed that Brooks was Lennox-Maxwell's real name. Brooks checked into the Palace Hotel, giving his name as T. C. D'Auquier from Paris. During the cross-country train trip, he had affected a phony French accent and told another passenger he was a brigadier-general in the French army. The handwriting of the man who checked into the Palace as D'Auquier, the handwriting of the man who signed his name on the train ticket as Hugh M. Brooks, and the handwriting of the man who'd posed as Lennnox-Maxwell at the Southern Hotel all matched each other.

Upon his arrival in San Francisco, Brooks promptly purchased a steerage ticket for Auckland, New Zealand, aboard the *City of Sydney*, and the ship sailed the next day, April 12. Authorities in New Zealand were promptly notified by telegram to be on the lookout for Brooks, and he was arrested when he disembarked at Auckland in early May. Two St. Louis detectives, carrying extradition papers signed by Missouri governor John S. Marmaduke and endorsed by President Grover Cleveland, left for New Zealand in early June and arrived late the same month. After a delay of almost a month, Brooks was surrendered to the St. Louis officers, and they brought him back to San Francisco, where a large crowd turned out to greet their arrival on August 11. When the detectives and their prisoner reached St. Louis on August 16, many curious onlookers again turned out to get a glimpse of the accused killer.

Brooks was indicted at the October 1885 term of the St. Louis Criminal Court, and his trial on a charge of first-degree murder was called on May 10, 1886, at the Four Courts Building. When testimony began a few days later, the prosecution paraded a gaggle of witnesses to the stand to build a strong circumstantial case against the defendant, showing that he was the same man who'd occupied Room 144 when Preller was killed, the same man who'd bought the trunks that were delivered to Room 144, the same man who'd written the note found in the zinc-covered trunk with the body, the same man who'd left hastily for San Francisco, and the same man who'd arrived there under the name of D'Auquier and sailed for New Zealand. One of the witnesses was the druggist who sold Brooks the chloroform, which medical experts testified was the means of death.

The most damaging state witness, however, was John McCullough, a railroad detective who'd been planted in jail under false charges to try to get information from Brooks. McCullough, who was the defendant's jail mate for forty-seven days, testified on May 24 that Brooks told him he killed Preller because he was low on funds and Preller refused to pay his way to New Zealand. Brooks said he "decided on account of his meanness to fix him." Preller had complained of a "private disease" and agreed to let Brooks perform an operation to relieve the pain. After injecting the patient with morphine to put him to sleep, Brooks used chloroform to try to kill him. Realizing he didn't have enough, he hurried out to get more and returned to finish the job.

The defense objected to the testimony of a jailhouse snitch and tried to get it excluded, but the motion was overruled.

When Brooks took the stand in his own defense on May 26, the largest crowd in the history of the St. Louis criminal courtroom packed the place, according the *Post-Dispatch*. The spectators "were not crowded, they were jammed."

During testimony that stretched into the next day, Brooks admitted using the chloroform on Preller, but he maintained that Preller's death was an accident, the result of an operation gone bad. Denouncing McCullough as a liar, Brooks said that Preller had suffered from painful and difficult urination and that he had diagnosed the cause as a stricture brought on by the patient's private disease or rather "private habit" (i.e. masturbation). Preller had agreed to let him insert a catheter into his urethra to relieve the condition. Brooks administered the first dose of chloroform and began the operation, but the patient was still wincing in pain. He rushed out to get more chloroform, but after he administered the second dose, Preller lapsed into unconsciousness and died. Brooks's effort to revive the patient failed, and he fled out of fear his story would not be believed.

And few people did believe it.

On cross-examination, the prosecution attacked Brooks as a chronic liar. He had adopted more than one fictitious identity. He represented himself to Preller and others as a doctor when he had no formal medical training. He told people that his father was dead and that he was soon to inherit a lot of money when his father was very much alive. He told Preller that he'd traveled extensively in Italy when he'd never set foot in Italy.

Brooks was obviously lying in this case, too, said the prosecution. If Preller's death was an accident as the defendant claimed, why did he steal the victim's money and belongings, stuff his nearly-nude body in a trunk, and try to stage the scene to look like a political assassination?

Finally, the state had Preller's body exhumed to further refute the defense's argument. An autopsy revealed that Preller had not suffered from a stricture and had not been treated with a catheter as Brooks had claimed. Of course, the defense argued that a postmortem so long after the fact was meaningless, but the mere fact that Brooks had impugned the character of the deceased by accusing him of "vile practices" was one more strike against him.

The judge's instructions to the jury on June 1 included the option of finding Brooks guilty of manslaughter if the jurymen felt Preller had died accidentally during an operation, but the jury came back on June 5, after several days of closing arguments and half a day of deliberation, with a verdict finding the defendant guilty of first-degree murder.

The defense's motion for a new trial was overruled in July, and Brooks, who was still calling himself Maxwell, was sentenced to hang on August 27, 1886. Unsuccessful appeals to both the Missouri Supreme Court and the US Supreme Court, along with a series of stays, delayed the execution for two years. It was finally set for August 10, 1888.

Early that morning, a large crowd began to gather around the city jail. "From all directions they came," said the *Post-Dispatch*, "a morbid, curious mass, to behold a fellow human being die." Many people climbed trees or looked out the windows of nearby tall buildings "straining their necks to catch a glimpse of the sickening scene" to be staged on the scaffold inside the surrounding stockade.

About 8:50 a.m., Brooks, accompanied by a Catholic priest, was led to the gallows, along with another condemned murderer, Henry Landgraf. Shortly before 9:00 a.m. Landgraf, who'd killed his sweetheart in a fit of rage, and the

Little Chloroformer, as Brooks was often called in the press, dropped through the chute at the same time.

"In fourteen minutes, the pride of the jail," said the *Post-Dispatch* in reference to Brooks, "had passed on into that world from which there is no return. Another will soon occupy his place in the city prison, and in a few years the public will have almost entirely forgotten that Maxwell ever lived. He and his crime will be numbered among the relics of the unrecalled past."

Unrecalled except by a few of us whose interest is still stirred 130 years later by one of the most sensational crime stories in Missouri history.

Chapter Ten

Turlington Tumbles
The Murderer of Sheriff Cranmer Hanged

On the morning of March 20, 1890, after a brakeman on the Missouri Pacific Railroad ejected John Oscar Turlington and Andy Temple from a train near Otterville, Missouri, Turlington took a pot shot at the brakeman. The railroad man came on to Sedalia to report the incident, and the two hooligans were arrested later the same day about four miles east of Sedalia in Pettis County. The twenty-six-year-old Turlington gave his name as William West, and Temple, who was a couple of years older, said his name was W. E. Smith.

Since the shooting had taken place in Cooper County, the pair were charged only with carrying concealed weapons, and they were tossed in jail at Sedalia. Turlington, though, also faced charges in Cooper County for felonious assault and was scheduled to be transferred there on the more serious charge as soon as his short term in Pettis County expired. Had the Missouri authorities been aware of Turlington's true identity and had they known him as well as the folks back in his native Weakley County, Tennessee, knew him, they might have taken more precautions.

Although of "good personal appearance," Turlington had a reputation in his home county as "one of the most abandoned and reckless desperadoes known to the annals of crime." His first serious trouble came when he got into a scuffle and cut another young man with a knife while in his early teens, and he was later rumored to have killed or attempted to kill at least one other man. He'd served two stints in the Tennessee State Penitentiary, and at one point he and his two brothers were all in prison at the same time. Sometime about 1883 or 1884, Turlington went to Indiana and worked a few months on a farm. He seemed to be a good employee, but when he got ready to leave, he slipped away, taking some clothes and money belonging to the farmer. About 1886, Turlington stole a horse from a black man in Weakley County but was never apprehended for the offense.

Shortly afterward, Turlington and another man broke into and robbed a store at Greenfield in Weakley County. Turlington was convicted of the crime and given a two-year sentence in the state penitentiary, where he was admitted in February 1887. Despite attempting to escape from the Nashville prison, he was turned loose early because of his mother's illness, but instead of going home to Ralston to see his sick mom, he headed west to add to his inventory of crimes. While in Texas, he wrote back to Weakley County threatening the local sheriff, who'd been instrumental in apprehending and convicting him of the store robbery.

On November 24, 1889, Turlington teamed up with Temple to rob an express train of the Missouri, Kansas and Texas Railroad near Pryor Creek, Indian Territory, taking $1,700. They were also suspected of helping several other bandits hold up a Wells-Fargo express car on the Atchison, Topeka and Santa Fe line near Berwyn (present day Gene Autry, Oklahoma) the very next night, but Turlington later confessed only to the Pryor Creek job.

Feeling that things were getting too hot for him in the West, Turlington, accompanied by Temple, came back east to Indiana, dividing his time during the winter of 1889-1890 between there and Kentucky. In the spring of 1890, he and Temple started back west once again, but they didn't make it across Missouri before landing in jail at Sedalia. While still incarcerated there, Turlington convinced a fellow inmate, seventeen-year-old Wes Hensley, to sneak a gun into him at the Cooper County Jail in Boonville once he was transferred, and young Hensley, who was due to be released soon, agreed to the desperate plan.

After serving their brief terms, Turlington and Temple were released from the Pettis County Jail in late May. Temple went free, but Turlington, still going by the name West, was taken to Cooper County to stand trial for shooting at the brakeman. According to Johnson's *History of Cooper County*, Turlington presented a pleasing personality, giving no appearance of being a hardened criminal, and Sheriff Thomas C. Cranmer, who was a warm-hearted man by nature, took sympathy on him. The fifty-four-year-old Cranmer arranged for legal representation for Turlington, and, with the sheriff's help, the defense got Turlington's charge reduced to a misdemeanor. By arrangement, he then pled guilty and received only a short term in the county jail.

Not short enough, though, to suit John Turlington.

On Friday, June 13, Wes Hensley came to Boonville and, using a ladder to reach Turlington's cell window in the Cooper County Jail, passed a weapon to the prisoner, as he'd promised back in Sedalia to do. The next night, about 7:00 p.m., while Turlington's cell door was open so that a porter could pick up his supper dishes and the sheriff stood in the corridor just outside the open door, Turlington walked out into the corridor and flourished a .44 revolver. "Old man, throw up your hands," he ordered. "I am going away from here."

When Sheriff Cranmer, instead of obeying the order, stepped back and reached for his pistol, Turlington opened fire and dashed for freedom. The bullet passed through Cranmer's arm and entered the left side of his abdomen. Severely wounded, the sheriff managed to get off two rounds at the fleeing prisoner but missed his target, as Turlington fled down some stairs and out a rear door.

The mortally wounded Cranmer managed to get the cell-block locked down so that other prisoners could not escape. He then staggered into his downstairs living quarters to report what had happened before collapsing. A large posse immediately formed, and Turlington was recaptured less than an hour after his escape.

After Turlington was brought back to Boonville, there was much talk of lynching him, but the dying sheriff requested that the people of Cooper County not take the law into their own hands. Cranmer succumbed the next morning after suffering through the night, and mob fever flared again. However, a Baptist minister and other influential citizens were able to convince the vigilantes who formed to honor the sheriff's wishes.

Shortly after Turlington's recapture, he revealed how he'd gotten the weapon with which he'd made his escape, and Hensley was arrested and lodged in jail at Sedalia. (He was later brought to Boonville after the fear of mob action abated.) Turlington also confessed his real identity, and he admitted that he and Temple had held up the train at Pryor Creek the previous fall.

In mid-July, Turlington and Hensley were formally indicted for first degree murder, but their cases were subsequently severed. While awaiting trial, Turlington exchanged letters with his mother, Ann Turlington, in Tennessee. In one of her letters to her son, Mrs. Turlington said she was praying for him, and she assured him that she loved him despite what he might have done. She said she would like to come and visit him but that she had no money to make the trip.

Turlington's trial began on July 23. Testifying in his own behalf, Turlington said he did not plan to kill Sheriff Cranmer and only shot him accidentally when he fell down as he was trying to escape. He said his mind was a blur and he really didn't remember the details except that the sheriff shot first and that he ran and fell as he was trying to get away. One of Turlington's cellmates also testified that the lawman fired first. However, Turlington admitted that his revolver was already cocked when he stepped out of his cell, and two other witnesses swore that the prisoner deliberately fired the first shot.

Sketch of John Oscar Turlington from *Sedalia Weekly Bazoo*.

On the afternoon of the 25th, the jury came back with a verdict of guilty after deliberating an hour and a half. Turlington was sentenced to hang, and the execution date was set for September 11. The case was appealed to the Missouri Supreme Court, however, and a stay of execution was granted pending the high court's ruling.

Turlington wrote a letter to his mother as soon as he got back to his jail cell after his trial ended. He broke the news to her that he had been sentenced to death. He said he was asking God to help her bear the news, and he assured her that he was more at peace with God than he'd ever been. He said he had not received a fair trial, but he referred his mother to his lawyer, William S. Shirk of Sedalia, if she wished to know the details.

On the evening of November 1, 1890, while still awaiting a ruling from the Missouri Supreme Court, Turlington escaped from the Cooper County Jail by placing a dummy in his bed and hiding in an empty, adjoining cell. After the guards, mistaking the dummy for a person, locked his cell for the night, he reached into his cell to retrieve his shoes, put them on, and slipped out through the corridors of the jail. Bloodhounds were soon on his trail, but the fugitive managed to elude the manhunt and make it out of Missouri.

Turlington's freedom, though, was once again short-lived. He was re-captured on November 11 at Caseyville, Kentucky, in the home of a family with whom he'd stayed briefly the previous winter. This time, though, the woman of the house got scared and mentioned her predicament to another man who was boarding with her. He informed local authorities, who came to the house and made the arrest.

Turlington spent a couple of nights in a Kentucky jail and then was brought back to Missouri, arriving in St. Louis on the morning of the 14th. Later the same day, a *St. Louis Post Dispatch* reporter called on him at the Four Courts Jail. The newspaperman described the prisoner as "a small man, rather slender in build and with a scanty beard covering his regular features. His eyes are gray and glitter in a determined manner. His general appearance, however, is that of a farmer, not a desperado."

The story of his first escape from the Cooper County Jail that Turlington told the reporter differed only slightly from what he'd said on the witness stand during his trial. He still insisted the sheriff had drawn his weapon and fired at him first as he was trying to escape, but he now admitted that his discharging of his revolver was not accidental. He said instead that he fired back at the sheriff in self-defense after he fell and the lawman was stalking toward him with his gun spitting lead.

Turlington had agreed to accompany the Kentucky officers who'd arrested him back to Missouri without resistance if they'd take him to Jefferson City instead of

Boonville, and he still hoped to be taken to the state capital. He wanted to go before the governor and ask for protection, because he was convinced he would be mobbed if he were taken back to Cooper County.

Informed that Wes Hensley had pleaded guilty to a reduced charge of murder in the second degree and received a sentence of ten years in the state prison, Turlington decried the verdict. "That boy ought not get a day in prison," he said. "He did not know what I wanted to do with that gun. Any way, he is not right in the head."

When the citizens of Weakley County read that Turlington stated, while in St. Louis, that he first went bad about five years ago, many of them had to smile, according to a special report from Dresden, the Weakley County seat. "Weakley County was long the scene of this criminal's crookedness," the report continued, "and there are plenty of men who will testify that Turlington has never been anything but a very depraved character ever since he arrived at the age of accountability."

Rather than escorting Turlington to Jefferson City as the prisoner requested, one of the Kentucky officers who had brought him to St. Louis took him back to Boonville in company with two Cooper County officers. When the party arrived on November 17, no mob greeted Turlington as he'd feared, and he was once again placed in the Cooper County Jail.

A little over a month later, on the night of December 20, Turlington escaped from the county jail yet again. Using a knife that had been slipped to him by another inmate, he'd started cutting a hole in the ceiling about ten days earlier. Working at night and covering his work back up each morning, he finally got a hole cut big enough to crawl through. Near midnight on the 20th or during the wee hours of the 21st, he stood on his cot and managed to pull himself up through the hole into the attic, taking along his blanket, which he'd fashioned into a rope. Groping along in the attic, he found a trap door leading onto the roof and then, securing the rope-blanket to a joist inside the trap door, he scaled down the side of the jail to the back yard. He stole a horse belonging to the new sheriff, Albert Hornbeck, from a nearby stable and rode rapidly to the area of Otterville, where he hid in a corn shock about dawn to rest.

He was recaptured later the same day, still in the corn shock. He was returned to Boonville and once again placed in the county jail. Hornbeck and other county officials received a lot of criticism, good natured and otherwise, as a result of Turlington's repeated escapes from their jail. A Sedalia reporter traveled to Boonville shortly after Turlington's latest caper and asked a Boonville newspaper editor whether he thought the county officers would let him into the jail to see Turlington. "They might not do that," the local editor replied wryly, "but they'll let you out damned easy."

Turlington's attitude turned belligerent after his latest recapture, as he started threatening his guards and exhibiting other aggressive behavior. Officials speculated he was only trying to get them to kill him, because he kept swearing that he would never hang.

Public sentiment, though, seemed to swing in Turlington's favor after his latest escapade. There was less inclination to want to see him hang, and some citizens expressed a certain admiration for him. One man even remarked that anyone who could escape from the same jail three times in so short a period should be turned loose.

The Missouri Supreme Court apparently didn't agree. The high court finally got around to considering Turlington's case in late January 1891. One of the main arguments that Turlington's lawyer advanced in his appeal was that, since Turlington was in jail on a misdemeanor charge, the sheriff should not have gone for his gun with the intent of using deadly force, and that, therefore, the prisoner was justified in shooting in self-defense. The Supreme Court justices, however, countered that the act of breaking jail was itself a felony and that the sheriff was under an obligation to prevent such an offense. Also, the fact that Turlington came out of his cell with a revolver that was already cocked showed premeditation. On January 27, the high court sustained the lower court's verdict and set the new execution date for March 6, 1891.

Immediately after receiving the news of the supreme court's decision, Turlington wrote a letter to his lawyer thanking him for everything he'd done. He said he didn't blame Shirk for the outcome, because the decision would have been the same regardless of who his lawyer was. Turlington said that, contrary to reports, he had not been threatening suicide and that he was bearing up as well as could be expected. Nonetheless, he asked Shirk to come and see him as soon as possible.

On February 22, Turlington wrote a letter to the public and sent it to the editor of the *Boonville Star* for publication. Comparing his death sentence to eternal damnation, he asked his readers to take the opportunity to escape their doom by accepting Christ the same way he had taken the opportunity to escape his death sentence by fleeing from the county jail. He urged them to step through the door of salvation into everlasting life the same way he had stepped through the jail door into freedom.

On March 6, the day of his execution, Turlington was brought out of his cell about ten o'clock in the morning. Without hesitation and with little support, he mounted the steps leading to the scaffold, which the *St. Louis Post Dispatch* described as a "very primitive man-killer, even for a gallows." A stockade had been erected around the scaffold, and only about forty people, mostly deputies and other officials, were allowed inside the enclosure. Turlington's only words to the witnesses were, "God bless and be with you all."

After Turlington was led to the trap, Sheriff Hornbeck and a deputy pinioned the condemned man's arms and covered his head, and a minister offered a brief prayer. The minister then whispered the Lord's Prayer to Turlington, who repeated it in a low voice.

The drop fell shortly after 10:00 a.m., and death was almost instantaneous.

"Turlington died game," one reporter said, almost with admiration. "His nerve never deserted him for an instant. He did not cry or exhibit any evidence of weakness. He surprised all by his steady nerve."

The evening before his execution, Turlington remarked that he didn't care what happened to his body because the Lord would take care of his soul. After the hanging, though, a local undertaker took charge of the body and had it buried in the Old City Cemetery (aka Sunset Hills) in Boonville.

Chapter Eleven

A Fitting End to a Dastardly Career
The Hanging of Thomas Williamson

About ten o'clock in the morning of May 26, 1890, law officers in Sedalia, Missouri, received a report that an old man had tried to commit suicide in a local public park by consuming a quantity of strychnine. Responding to the intelligence, the officers discovered fifty-four-year-old Thomas Williamson lying on the floor of an equipment building at the park, and they took him to the local Salvation Army barracks, where medical aid was administered.

Asked about his suicide attempt after he'd revived somewhat, Williamson responded, according to the *Sedalia Weekly Bazoo*, that "he was tired of living and wanted to meet his God."

However, later developments, said the *Bazoo*, gave "better reasons for Williamson's actions than 'tired of living.'" About 1:00 p.m. the same day, a man who lived two and a half miles southeast of Sedalia came to town and reported that one of his neighbors, Jeff Moore, had been found dead on his farm and that Williamson, who had recently been living with Moore, was suspected of the crime.

If the murder of Moore, as the *Bazoo* implied, was one of Williamson's "better reasons" for attempting suicide, then still later developments would uncover several additional "better reasons." In fact, "tired of killing" might have been a more apt explanation for Williamson's attempt to end his own life, because, as it turned out, he had a murderous record that stretched back almost twenty-five years and included three known victims and other suspected ones.

Thomas Andrew Williamson had grown up in Hopedale, Tazewell County, Illinois, and he served in the Union Army during the Civil War. After the war, he returned to Tazewell County and was working on Charles Koch's farm near Delavan in mid-July 1866 when he killed Koch and took possession of the farm, claiming Koch had sold it to him and left the country. The crime was discovered about a month later, and Williamson was subsequently arrested and charged with first degree murder. He was convicted and sentenced to hang in March of 1867, but the Illinois governor granted a reprieve. A mob organized to lynch Williamson after learning the news, but officers managed to protect the prisoner. The governor then commuted Williamson's sentence to twenty-one years in the Illinois State Penitentiary.

After serving slightly over half of his term, Williamson got out of prison in 1879, supposedly because of good behavior. One report at the time said he planned to move to Kansas and claim some land granted him by the government for his service during the war. However, he never settled in Kansas, although he did visit his parents and brother there during the mid-1880s.

In 1887, Williamson got married to Susan Reed Kirk in Vernon County, Missouri, just across the Kansas border from where his brother lived. The couple later moved to the Sedalia area, where Susan's brother, Matt Reed, lived. Williamson made his living working as a hired hand for various farmers in rural Pettis County.

Williamson and his wife were living on a farm about six miles northwest of Sedalia in the fall of 1889 when his wife disappeared, but nobody thought much about it at the time, because the couple had few acquaintances in the area. And Williamson explained to anyone who inquired that Susan had died while visiting relatives in Illinois. After his wife's disappearance, Williamson came to Sedalia for a while and then started working for Jeff Moore southeast of town in the early spring of 1890.

When a neighbor named August Brenicke called at the Moore place on Friday, May 25, to collect a debt, Williamson told him that he didn't know where Moore was. Brenicke and other neighbors grew suspicious the next day when they saw Williamson hauling dirt to the Moore farm with still no sign of Moore. On Monday morning they went to the farm and found Moore's body buried in a cellar beneath his house and Williamson nowhere to be seen. One of the neighbors brought the intelligence to Sedalia, and the suicidal Williamson, still recovering at the Salvation Army, was placed under guard.

Charles Moore, the son of Jeff Moore, had been missing for a couple of weeks, and after the father's body was found, it was feared that the son had been similarly dealt with. Further investigation at the Moore farm proved the fear well founded. The younger Moore's body was discovered buried face down about 200 yards from the house where Jeff Moore had been found.

A coroner arrived on the scene the afternoon of May 26, and his initial examination showed that both men had died from blows to the head with a sharp instrument. When the coroner returned to Sedalia later that day, Williamson was placed under arrest and removed from the Salvation Army to the Pettis County Jail. The next morning, a formal inquest concluded that both Jeff Moore and Charles Moore had come to their deaths at the hands of Thomas Williamson.

On the 28th, the body of Williamson's wife was found buried on the farm northwest of Sedalia where the couple had lived the previous fall. Given the likelihood that Williamson had killed the Moores and his previous statement that his wife had died in Illinois, Williamson was immediately suspected of having killed the woman, too, and a coroner's jury on the 29th officially charged him with the crime. It was feared that Williamson had also killed a boy who had worked for him on the farm, because the lad's whereabouts were unknown, but a search turned up no additional bodies.

A couple of days after Williamson's arrest, a *Sedalia Bazoo* reporter interviewed the prisoner at the county jail. Williamson was reluctant to talk at first, but he soon explained that his wife had died of the cramp colic and he'd simply buried her without ceremony because the couple had no friends in the area and he couldn't afford a coffin. He admitted he was present when both Jeff Moore and his son were killed, but he tried to lay the blame on Brenicke, the man who'd called at the Moore home to collect a debt.

Jeff Moore's estranged wife was arrested on suspicion of complicity with Williamson in the murder of her husband and stepson, but she was released shortly afterward.

On June 5, Williamson was taken to court for his preliminary hearing in the Moore murders, but he waived examination and was remanded to jail without bail to await the action of the grand jury.

The same day as his preliminary hearing, Williamson handed a written confession to Pettis County sheriff Ellis Smith taking full blame for the Moore murders and exonerating Brenicke. The prisoner said that he and Charlie Moore had been arguing off and on for a couple of weeks when the dispute grew heated one day about the middle of May while the two were clearing some ground with axes. Moore struck Williamson with the handle of his ax, and Williamson retaliated by striking Moore with the business end of his ax, knocking Moore down. Williamson then struck the fallen man a fatal blow.

A week later, Williamson and Jeff Moore got into a fuss about Charlie's disappearance, and Moore threw a chunk of wood at Williamson. Williamson retrieved his ax and hit Moore on the side of the head, knocking him down. He then killed Moore with a blow to the forehead.

Despite admitting to the murders of Jeff Moore and his son, Williamson maintained that he did not kill his wife. He continued to claim that she had gotten sick and died and that he'd buried her without a coffin because he was too poor to afford one. He gave out the story that she had died while visiting relatives just to stop people from asking questions about her.

On or near the same day Williamson gave his confession to Sheriff Smith, a letter arrived at the sheriff's office from Tazewell County, Illinois, from a man who'd grown up with Williamson. It gave a brief history of Williamson's family and outlined the circumstances of the murder Williamson had committed twenty-four years earlier. A *Weekly Bazoo* reporter called at the jail to get the prisoner's reaction to the letter, and Williamson confirmed that it was largely true.

Williamson was formally indicted on November 12, 1890, charged with first-degree murder in the deaths of the Moores. When the case was called on the 15th, Williamson's lawyers asked for and were granted a continuance until the February 1891 term of Pettis County Circuit Court.

When testimony in the trial began on February 5, Williamson's lawyers pursued an insanity defense. Testifying on his brother's behalf, Milton Williamson said the defendant had a bout of typhoid fever in 1858 that left him partially paralyzed on his right side and of unsound mind. Several men who'd served with Williamson in the Union Army testified that he was never given responsible duties in the military because he was incapable of carrying them out. He told wild stories and was considered weak minded and borderline insane. In an admission that perhaps undermined his own testimony, at least one of the defense witnesses admitted that Williamson had been prone to violence during his time in the army and had once threatened to kill a police officer who'd arrested him for brawling at Memphis.

The prosecutors countered that the defendant's state of mind many years ago was immaterial, and they placed several rebuttal witnesses on the stand, including the sheriff and his deputy, to testify that Williamson, except for the fantastic stories he told, was little different from other prisoners or other people in general.

Sketch of Thomas Williamson from *Sedalia Weekly Bazoo*.

Testimony in the case closed on the evening of February 6, and the jury came back the next morning with a verdict finding Williamson guilty of first-degree murder. Judge John E. Ryland pronounced a sentence of death by hanging on March 20, but the execution date was postponed when the defense took an appeal to the Missouri Supreme Court.

The high court took up the case at its April 1891 term. Although allowing that the defendant was not strong mentally, the justices found that his hiding of his victims, his secreting of their valuables, and his attempt at suicide when he was about to be discovered suggested that he knew right from wrong and that he recognized the enormity of his crimes. The justices, therefore, affirmed the judgment of the lower court and reset the execution date for August 21, 1891.

When the decision was announced in late June, a *Bazoo* reporter called at the Pettis County Jail to get

Williamson's reaction. Affecting disinterest, the prisoner said he didn't care what they did with him and that he would just as soon hang right now as any other time.

In late July, Williamson's lawyers, announcing that they had uncovered new evidence that would help their client, appealed to the Missouri Supreme Court for a new trial, and a petition circulated about the same time asking the Missouri governor to commute Williamson's sentence to life imprisonment. On the 29th, the high court issued a stay of Williamson's execution until the argument for a new trial could be heard.

The Missouri Supreme Court ruled on September 25 that a new trial would not be granted in Williamson's case, and his new execution date was set for October 31. On October 10, the petition for clemency, signed by a number of Pettis County citizens, was forwarded to Missouri governor David R. Francis. At the same time, Williamson reportedly wrote to the governor himself asking that the petition be denied, and a couple of days later Francis informed Pettis County officials that he would not interfere in the case.

Williamson then wrote out a story of his life, which was published in the *Bazoo* on the 18th. He confessed that his past life had been "one of crime and evil doings," and the story was largely a detailed accounting of his criminal activities, beginning with the theft of a plug of tobacco from his uncle when he was ten years old. Williamson readily admitted to a lifetime of thefts and other minor crimes, but, where accusations of murder were involved, he tried to shift blame or, in the case of Jeff Moore, justify the killing as self-defense.

As Williamson's execution drew near, interest in his case surged, and he was "visited daily by women of the better class," according to one newspaper report. On October 30, the eve of the execution, Williamson was baptized by a Catholic priest from Sedalia's St. Vincent's Church. He entertained several visitors that evening and ate a hearty dinner. That night he slept soundly for about four hours before awakening in the wee hours of Saturday morning, October 31.

The death walk began at 9:45 a.m., and Williamson mounted the scaffold with a slow but steady step. The condemned man, who had admitted the evening before that he "ought to have been hung thirty years ago," gave a very brief speech admonishing young men not to follow his example.

Sheriff Smith sprang the trap at 10:02 a.m., dropping Williamson through the chute with a neck-snapping jerk, and he was pronounced dead at 10:18. The *St. Louis Post Dispatch* called the execution "one of the most satisfactory hangings that has ever occurred in the West." The *Bazoo* concurred that the execution, which employed the same rope used to hang Turlington at Boonville earlier in the year, was "a success in every particular." The local newspaper also added that the hanging was a "fitting end to a dastardly career."

Williamson's body was taken down, placed in a cheap coffin, and removed to a local undertaker's parlor. Only lawmen, jurymen, Williamson's spiritual advisor, and a few other invited guests had witnessed the hanging, but over 5,000 people, curious to see the body, paraded through the mortuary afterward. A funeral was held at 3:00 p.m. that afternoon, and the body was then buried in a local potter's field.

Chapter Twelve

The Death of Lula Noel,
America's Knoxville Girl

I met a little girl in Knoxville, a town we all know well,
And every Sunday evening, out in her home I'd dwell,
We went to take an evening walk about a mile from town,
I picked a stick up off the ground and knocked that fair girl down.

She fell down on her bended knees for mercy she did cry,
Oh Willy dear don't kill me here, I'm unprepared to die,
She never spoke another word, I only beat her more,
Until the ground around me within her blood did flow.

I took her by her golden curls and I drug her round and around,
Throwing her into the river that flows through Knoxville town,
Go down, go down, you Knoxville girl with the dark and rolling eyes,
Go down, go down, you Knoxville girl, you can never be my bride.

"Knoxville Girl" as recorded by the Louvin Brothers

Twenty-three-year-old Mary Lula "Louie" Noel was
staying with her married sister, Laura Holly, in Indian
Territory in the summer of 1892 when she met a young man
named William Simmons, who was temporarily hiding out in
the territory to avoid paying a fine for flourishing a weapon
and resisting a law officer in Joplin, Missouri. After striking
up a tentative romance with Lula, the twenty-five-year-old
Simmons soon returned to Joplin to face the consequences
for his minor scrape with the law, and the Hollys also moved
back to Missouri and took up residence about a mile
southeast of Lanagan on the north side of Cowskin Creek
(i.e. Elk River) just across the river from Lula and Laura's

parents. (Interestingly, the Holly place was the former farm of Garland Mann, who had been killed in 1885 by vigilantes who broke into the Neosho jail, where he was being held on a charge of murdering Dr. Albert Chenoweth in Pineville two years earlier.)

Simmons, who worked for the Picher White Lead Works in Joplin, continued to court Miss Noel after returning to Missouri. They exchanged letters, and Simmons trekked to McDonald County on at least one occasion in the fall of 1892 to visit the beautiful Miss Noel.

Lula's grandfather was the founder of the town of Noel, and her family was one of the most prominent and wealthy in McDonald County. Her father, William Noel, was McDonald County assessor-elect. He and his wife, Susan Noel, opposed the match between their lovely, well-bred daughter and the wayward Simmons.

But Lula, despite arguing with Simmons on several occasions, was seemingly struck on the young man, and rumor had it the couple were planning to marry. In November, shortly after Simmons had been to visit her, Lula wrote to him saying that she was sorry he had gone, that she felt very lonesome, and that she hoped he would come back to see her soon. She asked him to burn the letter after he read it so that her family members might not learn of it.

On Monday, December 5, Lula left her parents' home and crossed the river to stay with her sister Laura. On December 7, Simmons took a train from Joplin to McDonald County to rendezvous with his sweetheart, arriving at the Holly place later that day. At some point during Simmons's stay, he and Lula argued again, and Lula tried to break their engagement, saying she wanted him to leave and not return. However, they apparently reconciled and were on good terms by the time Laura and her husband, Sidney, left on Saturday morning, December 10, to visit relatives, because Lula declined an invitation to accompany the couple. Simmons planned to go back to Joplin later that day, and Lula said she would stay with him until he left and then either return to her parents' home on the other side of Cowskin Creek or else stay with relatives north of the creek if the water was too high to cross.

Simmons returned to Joplin as planned, but Lula didn't show up at her parents' house and wasn't at the Holly residence when Laura and Sidney came home on Sunday. The young woman also could not be located at the home of any of her relatives in the Lanagan area. It was thought she might have accompanied Simmons to Joplin and gone on to Webb City to stay with an uncle there, as she sometimes did, and a letter was dispatched on Monday or Tuesday to the uncle inquiring whether Lula was at his house. When a negative answer came back later in the week, alarm for Lula's safety heightened.

On Friday, December 16, Sidney Holly and Lula's father traveled to Joplin to find out whether Simmons might know anything of her whereabouts. When they located him on the street and told him Lula was missing, he said he didn't know where she was. He'd last seen her about four o'clock Saturday afternoon when he left the Holly place to walk to Lanagan and catch a train for Joplin. Before he left, Simmons said, he asked Lula what she was going to do, and she said she was going home. When he asked how she was going to get across the river, Lula told him her cousin, who lived nearby on the north side of the stream, would row her across.

Simmons didn't seem overly concerned by the disappearance of his girlfriend, but Holly and Mr. Noel thought he appeared nervous during his conversation with them. When a carriage came driving down the street, Simmons asked why the carriage was coming toward them, as though he thought authorities might be coming for him. At one point he asked, "You don't suppose the fool girl jumped in the river and drowned herself, do you?" It struck the two men as strange that the only suggestion Simmons offered about Lula's possible whereabouts was an intimation that she might have committed suicide.

With their fears completely aroused after questioning Simmons, Holly and Noel returned to McDonald County and organized a thorough search for Lula the next day, Saturday, December 17, exactly one week after her disappearance. Over forty neighbors joined in the hunt. The searchers scoured the hills between the Holly home and Lanagan first, and then, taking a cue from Simmons's suggestion that Lula might have drowned, they turned their attention to the nearby river. Finally, about two o'clock in the afternoon, Lula's body was found in a narrow place in the creek, where her clothes had caught on a willow branch or root that projected into the water. The narrow was about a quarter to a half mile downstream from the Holly place near a ford Lula would have crossed to get to her parents' home.

The body was pulled from the stream and taken to the Noel residence, where an inquest was held Saturday night under the direction of McDonald County coroner J. E. Edelen. The examination found three or four bluish marks resembling fingerprints on one of Lula's cheeks, and another bluish mark on the other cheek resembling a thumbprint, as if an assailant had covered her mouth in an attempt to stifle her screams. There were also fingerprints on her throat and a mark over the right eye near the temple. There was a heavy bruise at the back of the head near the base of the skull, as though the victim had been struck by a blunt instrument, and the neck was broken.

The coroner's inquest ruled that Lula came to her death as a result of foul play, and Williams Simmons was immediately suspected of the crime. Two sets of tracks, one apparently belonging to a man and the other to a woman, were found leading from the Holly home to a nearby haystack, where signs of a struggle were found. Upon later comparison, the footprints of the man were found to fit the size of Simmons's shoes, and the footprints of the woman matched Lula's shoes.

Heavy footprints led from the haystack to the river and lighter ones by the same foot led away from the river, suggesting that a burden had been carried from the haystack to the river and dumped in the water. A blue fascinator was attached to Lula's hair, but the hat that went with the fascinator was found lying on a bed in the Holly house, further suggesting that she was killed at or near the house and carried to the river.

In reporting the crime, the *St. Louis Post-Dispatch* observed that Lula was "a very pretty girl," and another report described her as "extremely handsome" with "lady like manners" and "a favorite with all who knew her." Lula was buried on Sunday the 18th.

A warrant for the arrest of William Simmons was issued the same day and placed in the hands McDonald County sheriff W. W. Bacon. Traveling to Joplin, Bacon was unable to locate the suspect; so he turned the warrant over to Joplin city marshal J. J. Cofer and went back to McDonald County. About 4:00 p.m. on Monday, December 19, a US marshal and a city policeman went to Simmons's place of employment, the Picher White Lead Works. Simmons saw the officers coming and hid in a boxcar before they could nab him, but he was found later that evening at his brother's home in Joplin. He appeared to be preparing to take flight, but this time he was apprehended before he could abscond. The captive, who stoutly protested his innocence, was described at the time as a "tough character" who was "well known to the police." He stood about five feet and nine inches tall, weighed about 180 pounds, and was "fairly good looking," with a dark complexion and a brown mustache.

At the city jail in Joplin on Monday night, Simmons told a news reporter and other witnesses that he "was no more guilty of this crime than you men are." He said he would no more harm Lula than he would his own mother and that he and Lula had always gotten along well. He admitted he'd been dodging law officers of late because of the scrape he'd gotten into about a year earlier but that he had never been charged with a serious crime. He said the last time he'd seen Lula was on the afternoon of December 10 when they'd left the Holly home together. After a short distance, they parted, with him going toward Lanagan and Lula walking in the opposite direction.

Simmons spent the night in the Joplin City Jail, and Sheriff Bacon arrived the next day, December 20, to take charge of the prisoner. Since McDonald County had no jail at the time, Bacon took Simmons to Neosho and lodged him in the Newton County Jail.

On Christmas Day, Lula's body was exhumed for a more thorough autopsy. The examiners found the same bruising about the head and face that Dr. Edelen noticed during the original inquest. In addition, they found that the lungs and stomach were free of water, suggesting that death had occurred before Lula's body was dumped in the river.

Simmons's preliminary hearing was scheduled for Tuesday, December 27, and a large crowd gathered in Pineville that morning in anticipation of the event. Because excitement over Lula's violent death had been running so high in McDonald County, it was thought the courts would probably be "saved the trouble of a trial" if the prisoner was brought to the county seat as planned. To thwart the feared mob action, Henry Prater, the justice of the peace who'd issued the arrest warrant, arranged for Simmons to be brought to his home near Lanagan for the hearing rather than taken to his office in Pineville, where Prater usually transacted official business. Accordingly, Simmons was escorted on an 11:00 a.m. train to Lanagan, where the defendant waived preliminary examination, and he was returned to Neosho on a 1:35 p.m. train before the restless crowd in Pineville knew what was happening. When they learned of the ruse, it caused "quite an ill feeling" toward the officers involved, especially Justice Prater.

Simmons was indicted for first-degree murder at the February 1893 term of the McDonald County Circuit Court in Pineville. Although the fever pitch of excitement surrounding Lula's death had died down some by this time, prejudice against Simmons was still strong enough that the judge granted his application for a change of venue to Newton County. He was then taken back to Neosho to await trial.

The defendant was arraigned at the May term of Newton County Court, and his trial began on May 30 in front of a comparatively small courtroom audience. Between fifty and sixty witnesses took the stand for the state and about half that number for the defense. Many of the witnesses were people involved in the search for Lula's body or officers involved in Simmons's arrest. In addition, a neighbor of the Hollys said she had heard the seemingly distressed cry of a woman coming from the direction of the haystack on the day of Lula's disappearance, and another state witness, Anderson Jobe, testified that he met Simmons walking hurriedly toward Lanagan late on the afternoon in question and that his clothes were wet from the waist down.

Simmons claimed he had met Jobe on the Wednesday of his arrival in McDonald County, not the Saturday of his departure, and the defense produced witnesses to back up his story, because Jobe had said it was rainy on Saturday afternoon and the other witnesses testified that it was rainy on Wednesday but clear on Saturday. In addition, the defense called its own witnesses who had seen Simmons walking toward Lanagan on Saturday afternoon, but, unlike Jobe, they said the young man was not acting suspiciously at the time. As for the tracks leading from the Holly home to the haystack, Simmons's lawyers pointed out that the size of the footprints were a match for Sidney and Laura Holly as well as for the defendant and the deceased, and the defense produced a witness who said Laura had admitted she and her husband made the tracks a day or two before Lula's disappearance.

Each side also trotted out expert witnesses to testify as to the cause of death. The prosecution, of course, argued that Lula had died from blunt force trauma or by having her neck broken and was then placed in the river. The defense experts, on the other hand, maintained that there was no definite proof that Lula had come to her death through foul play and that the lack of water in her lungs, upon being exhumed eight days after her death, was not absolute proof that she was killed before entering the water.

The *Neosho Times* observed near the end of the proceedings that the strongest evidence of Simmons's guilt seemed to be his suspicious behavior in the immediate wake of the crime and his attempt to evade officers when they came to arrest him. However, the *Times* felt that the state's case suffered from the prosecutors' failure to establish a clear motive, and it was not proven beyond a reasonable doubt that a crime had even occurred. It was the general opinion, added the *Times*, that Simmons would probably not be convicted, although many people would always believe he was guilty.

The trial did, indeed, end without a conviction. The jury deliberated throughout the weekend of June 10-11, and when they came back on Monday the 12th, the jurors announced that they could not reach a verdict. They were reportedly split two for conviction and ten for acquittal. The judge declared a mistrial.

Simmons's retrial came off at the November 1893 term of Newton County Court. The evidence presented differed very little from that given at the first trial. Unlike their position at the previous trial, however, prosecutors allowed that there was at least the possibility that Lula had been killed on impulse. They adopted a theory of the crime that Simmons had killed Lula while attempting to "ruin her" and that the murder might have been committed during the struggle, without deliberation. The defense, on the other hand, suggested that the cause of death was suicide by drowning or that, if a crime had been committed, it was done by someone who was jealous of the attentions Lula had been paying to Simmons.

Taking the stand in his own defense, Simmons testified, according to the *Neosho Times*, in a "clear and strong" voice and "without any hesitation." The state cross-examined him thoroughly but "failed to confuse or entangle him."

At the end of testimony, the prosecution asked for an option of finding the defendant guilty of second-degree murder as well as first degree, and the judge so instructed the jurors. They retired on Thursday evening, December 7, deliberated throughout the day on Friday, and finally came back on Saturday morning with a verdict of murder in the second degree. Punishment was set at ten years in the state penitentiary.

A defense motion for a new trial was overruled on December 14, and Simmons's lawyers immediately filed a motion for an appeal to the Missouri Supreme Court. It was allowed with the provision that the defense had to file its bill of exceptions within sixty days. Among the defense objections were the fact that Simmons had been forced to give up his shoes as evidence, which amounted to self-incrimination, and the fact that testimony tending to show Lula had previously threatened suicide was not allowed. The high court, however, declined to hear the appeal, because the bill of exceptions was filed on February 13, 1894, one day after the allotted sixty-day period expired. The sentence of the Newton County court was, therefore, confirmed on November 5, 1894, and Simmons was committed to the state prison in Jefferson City on December 20, 1894. He was discharged on June 15, 1901 under the three-fourths rule that allowed early release for good behavior.

An interesting footnote to the Lula Noel case is that it became the inspiration for the American version of "Knoxville Girl," a well-known folk song popularized in 1956 by the Louvin Brothers. The original version of the song dates back to England many years earlier, but Lula Noel was America's Knoxville girl.

Chapter Thirteen

Go In or Have Blood
The Murder of John and Mary Stull

By all accounts, John Stull was a compassionate person who was always willing to help out his neighbors. Little did he know that his kindness would end up getting him and his mother killed.

During the late 1880s and early 1890s, Stull lived with his elderly mother, Mary Hughes, and his two young children in a crude, two-room house at Salt River Switch, a stop along the Hannibal to St. Louis Railroad about three miles north of New London in Ralls County, Missouri. Stull's wife had been dead several years, his mother was feeble and had poor eyesight, and his children were too young to work. Stull was the family's sole support, and, according to later testimony, he worked "hard to make an honest living for himself and helpless family, always bearing the name of an honest, upright, and peaceable old citizen."

In the spring of 1893, John Nelson and his wife, Lavinia, moved to the Salt River Switch area and pitched their tent about three hundred and fifty feet south of the Stull home. A short time later, Nelson's mother and stepfather, Samuel Minor, showed up in a covered wagon and parked it near Nelson's tent. Minor and his wife lived in the wagon but cooked their meals on Nelson's stove and ate from his table.

After a while, though, Nelson and his wife had a falling-out with the Minors and wouldn't let them cook on their stove or eat at their table. Neglected by her son, Mrs. Minor fell ill, but rather than help her out, Nelson and his wife pulled the wagon, with the mother in it, away from their tent and left it in a muddy, swampy area nearby.

Neighbors, including John Stull, came to Mrs. Minor's aid, and Stull agreed in late July, at the suggestion of Sam Minor and some of the other neighbors, to shelter Nelson's mother at his house and care for her there. He gave Mrs. Minor his best bed, and his mother, Mrs. Hughes, tended to the needs of their houseguest. Although Mrs. Minor was sick enough for a local doctor to pay a house call at the Stull place, Nelson and his wife never visited at all nor expressed any concerns about her welfare.

On Wednesday, August 2, 1893, while Stull's sister was visiting in the Stull home, her little boy and Stull's seven-year-old son, Willie, wandered in their play over to the Nelson tent, where Nelson enticed them into fighting each other. Stull's sister, seeing what was going on, sent Stull's daughter, fourteen-year-old Mary, over to the Nelson place to bring the children home. When the girl arrived to summon her brother and cousin home, Nelson abused her, calling her vile names.

Informed of what had happened, Stull confronted Nelson on Thursday as he was passing on the public road near Nelson's tent. Stull demanded to know why Nelson had mistreated the little boys and verbally abused his daughter. "Quite a war of words ensued," according to later court documents. Nelson cursed Stull, and Stull told Nelson and his wife he didn't want anything more to do with them and for them never to come to his place.

Although neither Nelson nor Lavinia had ever shown any inclination to visit Stull's home, Stull's decree banning them from his place made them determined to go there in defiance. On Friday, the day after the argument, Nelson told one of his neighbors that Stull had prohibited him from coming into his yard but that he "was going in if he had to bore his way in."

True to his word, Nelson showed up at the Stull house on Saturday morning, August 5, carrying a British bull dog revolver, with Lavinia by his side. They walked into the house uninvited but stayed less than five minutes when they realized Stull was not home, scarcely staying long enough to check on Nelson's sick mother.

The Nelsons went north along the railroad to a neighbor's camp, where they spent the better part of the day vocally abusing Stull and vowing that, as soon as he came home from work, they were going back to his place to "go in or have blood."

Shortly before 6 p.m. the Nelsons started back to Stull's place with Nelson carrying the revolver. Lavinia picked up a piece of iron as she and her husband approached the Stull home. Stull, who'd just gotten home, was sitting on the doorstep and saw the couple walking toward his yard. He told them to stay out, but they stepped through an opening in the fence and kept on coming.

Hearing the commotion, Stull's mother stepped outside carrying a dish cloth in one hand and a case knife in the other, which she'd been using to fix supper. About that moment Lavinia Nelson struck Stull with the piece of iron she was holding. In return, Stull slapped her with his hand. Nelson then fired a shot at Stull, but it missed and struck Mary Hughes instead. She fell "speechless and almost lifeless, with a bullet hole in her head and her brains running out on the ground profusely," and she died very shortly.

After the first shot, Nelson fired again, this time striking Stull in the abdomen. Nelson and his wife then turned and left, with Stull staggering after them until they reached the top of the nearby railroad grade, where Stull fell on the track.

Here, according to the subsequent testimony of nearby witnesses, Nelson hallooed that he had "shot the damned son of a bitch." Two men who'd heard the shots hurried to the scene and tried to disarm Nelson. He threatened to shoot one of them, but they were able to take his weapon and summon help.

Stull died the next day, about the same time Sheriff Charles Weaver lodged Nelson and his wife in the Ralls County Jail at New London. When he was arrested, Nelson bragged to the sheriff that, although he didn't mean to hurt the old lady, he "didn't care a damn if he did kill Stull" and that, if he had it to do over, he would do it again.

Nelson and his wife were jointly indicted for the double murder at the August term of Ralls County Circuit Court, Nelson as the principal and Lavinia as an accessory. The case was continued until March of 1894, at which time Lavinia applied for and obtained a severance of her case from her husband's.

When Nelson's case came up in July, his attorneys applied for and obtained a change of venue to neighboring Marion County. His trial for the first degree murder of John Stull began at Palmyra in October 1894. The prosecution introduced a number of witnesses who testified of Nelson's mistreatment of his mother, of his newfound determination to visit her once Stull had banned him from his property, of his threats toward Stull on the day of the murders, and of his boasting about the incident after it was over. The prosecution also relied heavily on Stull's dying statements and on eight-year-old Willie Stull's eyewitness testimony.

The defense claimed that Nelson fired the first shot only after Stull had struck Lavinia without provocation and that he then shot Stull only because Stull was coming at him with a knife. No knife, however, was found on Stull or anywhere near where he fell. Nelson also claimed he and his wife had no quarrel with Stull prior to the fatal encounter, despite ample prosecution testimony to the contrary. The defense also said that Lavinia Nelson was seriously hurt by the blow or blows Stull delivered to her and that she almost miscarried as a result. Again abundant testimony to the contrary showed that she was seen walking around the neighborhood, going from place to place the evening after the murders, exhibiting no signs of injury, and she safely delivered her baby about three months later while in jail.

Sketch of John Nelson from *Marion County Herald.*

Nelson's trial ended in a hung jury, eleven jurors voting for conviction and one holding out for acquittal. A new trial was set for April of 1895 at Palmyra. Willie Stull, now nine years old, was again the star witness for the prosecution. He seemed "exceedingly bright," according to one newspaper report, and was "cool as a cucumber" in relating how the Nelsons had come into the Stull yard against his father's orders and how John Nelson had shot and killed both his father and his grandmother. On Thursday night, April 11, the jury came back after several hours of deliberation with a verdict finding the defendant guilty of murder in the first degree. The judge pronounced a sentence of death by hanging, but the execution was stayed when the defense appealed the verdict to the Missouri Supreme Court.

Lavinia Nelson's trial as an accessory to first degree murder began at New London in late April 1895, and the jury came back with a not guilty verdict on May 3. The verdict surprised many observers who felt that Lavinia was just as guilty as her husband, but sympathy for the woman and her fifteen-month-old child, who'd been born a few months after her arrest, played a role in the outcome of the trial. The little boy was allowed to toddle over to Willie Stull as the Stull lad was giving his testimony, and such antics, it was thought, aroused the sympathy of the jury. After her acquittal, Lavinia utterly deserted her husband, taking no interest in his case and refusing even to answer the letters he wrote to her.

The Supreme Court of Missouri took up the John Nelson case in January of 1896. One of the defense's primary arguments was that Willie Stull's testimony should not have been allowed, since he was too young to be a competent witness, but the high court disagreed. Calling Nelson's crime a "deliberate and most atrocious murder," the justices announced a decision on the 21st affirming the verdict of the lower court and setting Nelson's hanging for February 28, 1896, at Palmyra.

On February 23, five days before his date with death, Nelson dictated a letter to be sent to his cousin in Illinois. A fellow inmate wrote the letter, and it was later published in a Palmyra newspaper. Nelson informed his cousin that he had joined the Catholic Church on December 26, 1895, and much of the letter was devoted to citing Bible verses.

Nelson's hanging was scheduled for eleven o'clock on the morning of Friday the 28th, and by 10:30 a small crowd of about fifty invited spectators had gathered inside the stockade surrounding the gallows that stood just outside and below the condemned man's cell at the Marion County Jail. Nelson was drinking a glass of water, and when he looked out to see the small crowd, he tossed the remainder of the water through his window and smiled mischievously to see the startled reactions of those on whom the drops fell.

Afterward he called for a cigar and then sent word to reporters that he was enjoying his smoke. His facade of aplomb shattered a few minutes later when Sheriff Ed Pratt came into his cell to escort him to his doom. Nelson burst into tears and begged to be given a little more time, but Pratt was quickly able to calm him down. Leaning on the arm of his spiritual advisor, Nelson put on an impassive face as he followed the sheriff outside and up the stairs to the gallows. Given an invitation to speak, Nelson said he had nothing to say except that he was innocent. He was then positioned over the trap door, and the preparations were quickly made. The sheriff pulled the lever to spring the trap, and Nelson shot through the opening into eternity just a minute and a half after he'd ascended the scaffold.

The body was cut down after twenty minutes and taken into the jail, where it was placed in a coffin provided by the local Catholic Church. Although, according to the *Palmyra Spectator*, the crowd that gathered for the hanging fest was comparatively small and only a limited number of observers were allowed inside the stockade, a lot of people thronged into the jail to see the body after it was cut down. And although Nelson was buried in a Palmyra cemetery two and a half hours after the execution, the scaffold was allowed to stand until Saturday night "for the benefit of sight-seers."

Chapter Fourteen

The Tramp Became a Demon
The Lynching of Thomas Larkin

After Alice Gammon, a deaf girl whose age was given as anywhere from ten to thirteen, was brutally assaulted by an adult white male on Wednesday, September 2, 1896, at Rhineland, Missouri, a man calling himself Thomas Larkin was quickly identified as the likely assailant and was held under guard that night at the Rhineland Hotel awaiting transfer to the Montgomery County seat at Danville. The attack on Alice, who'd always been "an object of pity" in the community because of her disability, threw the normally law-abiding German people of Rhineland into a rage, and many of them gathered throughout the evening near the hotel plotting vengeance against Tom Larkin. Still, the crowd was slow to violence, said the *St. Louis Post-Dispatch*, and "the mob reluctantly permitted Larkin to live."

At least for that night.

But as more details about the brutal attack on Alice were made public and more evidence against the suspect was turned up, the people were aroused to a fever pitch.

Alice, along with several other young girls, worked in a canning factory a short distance outside Rhineland. After putting in a day's work on the 2nd, she left the factory by herself about 6:00 p.m. and started on foot to her home a half mile away. Meanwhile, Larkin, "a tramp mechanic," had arrived in Rhineland by rail early the same morning with two companions, and they spent the day repairing gasoline stoves for whoever would hire them. Late in the afternoon, Larkin left his two companions in Rhineland and walked out into the surrounding countryside alone.

Shortly after leaving the factory, Alice noticed someone following her. As she neared her home, the path she was on took her into a thicket of woods, and halfway through it, the man who'd been following her made a rush toward her. Seizing Alice, he threw her to the ground and smothered her cries with her skirts. The girl struggled and fought, as the assailant, in the words of the *Post-Dispatch*, "clutched her throat and pressed his sharp finger nails into the soft white flesh until the blood came.

"Failing in his design," the St. Louis newspaper continued, "the tramp became a demon." He pulled a knife from his pocket and stabbed Alice, then withdrew the bloody blade and plunged it into her flesh again.

"Still balked in his purpose," Larkin released the girl and dashed into the woods.

Weak from the attack, Alice staggered and crawled to her nearby home. It was 7:30 p.m. when she dragged herself into the house, faint and still bleeding from her wounds. She told her eight-year-old sister what had happened, and the little girl raced to fetch William Dixon, the town constable, who, in turn, summoned a local physician.

After the doctor treated Alice, she revived enough to describe her assailant. She said he wore a derby hat, had black curly hair and a sandy mustache, and was missing the first finger of his left hand. Constable Dixon found a man answering the description on the platform of the railroad depot about 300 yards from the scene of the assault, except that he wasn't wearing a hat like the one the girl had described. The suspect stoutly denied having attacked the girl and tried to lay the blame instead on one his fellow mechanics. The second man did have a derby hat, but he explained that the suspect had asked him to switch hats after returning from the countryside.

Besides, the missing finger was convincing evidence. In addition, the constable took the suspect to Alice's house, and she positively identified him. She said she was sure because the man's face had been etched on her memory while he was attacking her.

Since Rhineland was a small village with no jail, Dixon escorted the suspect to the town's only hotel and placed him in one of the rooms, where the constable and two deputies guarded him. The prisoner identified himself as Thomas Larkin from Chicago, although other reports said he was from New York. He was described as about thirty years old, of medium height, and weighing about 150 pounds.

Larkin had scarcely been confined when word spread that the doctor attending Alice had said her wounds were likely fatal and that, even if she recovered, she would be scarred for life. The people of Rhineland began collecting near the hotel, discussing the attack on Alice, and plotting to take Larkin from his guards so that they might visit a swift vengeance upon him. The deliberate Germans took several hours talking over the matter, while Larkin, aware of the gathering mob, moaned and quaked with fear in his hotel room, begging his guards to protect him from the ominous horde.

After midnight, the crowd, now swollen in numbers, began to grow impatient. According to the *Post-Dispatch*, the people were "rapidly approaching a state where the presence of a leader would have sufficed to end Larkin's life" when a freight train pulled into the nearby railway station. The interruption granted Larkin a temporary reprieve, but after the train pulled away from Rhineland, the mob broke into a hardware store and retrieved a rope.

It was about 3:00 a.m. on the morning of September 3 when they started back toward the hotel with the rope. Constable Dixon came out in front of the hotel to plead with them, and cooler heads among the crowd also counseled against rash action. Some felt the mob should not lynch Larkin as long as there was hope that Alice would recover, and some still had a bit of doubt as to Larkin's guilt. Thus, the throng finally agreed to disband

For the time being, anyway.

Most of the would-be lynchers, however, lingered near the hotel, and after daylight more citizens from the surrounding countryside began pouring into town. By mid-morning, the town was full of people, and Constable Dixon and one of his deputies, realizing that mob fever would likely flare again, tried to take Larkin from the hotel so they could escort him to Danville. The crowd, though, would not let them pass and forced them to retreat into the hotel once again.

Realizing the dire circumstances, Dixon telegraphed for the Montgomery County sheriff. While the constable awaited the sheriff's arrival from Danville, events continued to unfold that further inflamed the mob gathered around the Rhineland Hotel. Someone reported that he had heard Larkin make indecent proposals to two women who departed on the east-bound train the previous day before the attack on Alice Gammon.

Next, a section hand, employed at Rhineland by the Missouri, Kansas and Texas Railroad, came forward to declare that he had witnessed the assault on Alice and that Thomas Larkin was the guilty party. The witness said he had been walking along the railroad track east of the depot when he saw Larkin struggling with the girl in the edge of the woods north of the track. He said he was afraid to intervene for fear of what "the fiend" might do to him but that he hurried to report the incident to Constable Dixon, who had advised him not to tell his story to others because of the exciting effect it would have.

By the time the sheriff arrived in the late afternoon, the crowd at Rhineland had grown so large and so indignant that the lawman was unable to remove the prisoner as he had planned. His presence, however, helped deter the would-be lynchers from trying to act during the daytime.

About ten o'clock that night, however, word reached the mob that Alice Gammon was dying. Whether the report was valid and the girl did, in fact, later die is not clear, but the mere rumor of Alice's impending death was sufficient to incite the horde to action.

Eight or ten masked men, one of them toting a long rope, advanced out of the crowd and started battering the front door. The sheriff, the constable, and a deputy were on the other side of the door, and when it yielded, the officers put up a stiff resistance, knocking one of the besiegers down. The other vigilantes, though, overpowered the lawmen and quickly located Larkin. They tossed the rope around his neck with a running noose and half-dragged, half-carried him outside as he struggled for his life. The mob took him to a spot about 200 yards east of the railway station and just north of the track, which was near the woods where Alice Gammon had been attacked. By the time the gang reached the preselected site, Larkin's clothes had nearly been torn from his body and his face was scratched and begrimed from contact with the ground.

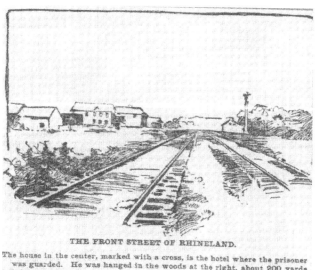

THE FRONT STREET OF RHINELAND.

The house in the center, marked with a cross, is the hotel where the prisoner was guarded. He was hanged in the woods at the right, about 200 yards below the town.

Scene at Rhineland, where Larkin was held and lynched. *St. Louis Post-Dispatch.*

The other end of the rope was thrown over a limb of an oak tree at the edge of the woods, and Larkin, too exhausted to stand on his own, was stood up beneath the limb. Asked if he had anything to say, he declared, "I am an innocent man."

He had scarcely uttered the words before the howling mob grasped the rope and drew him up. They left him dangling beneath the limbs of the tree for passengers and crew to see as they passed on the nearby railroad tracks. When a freight train went through Rhineland after daylight on the morning of September 4, about seven hours after the lynching, Larkin's body was still swinging from the limb, and a number of curious onlookers were standing nearby gawking at the grisly sight.

The body was cut down later that morning, and the coroner held an inquest, which yielded the predictable verdict: that Tom Larkin had come to his death at the hands of parties unknown.

In mid-December, over three months after the lynching, J. J. Kane of East Albany, New York, showed up in Montgomery County saying he thought the man who'd been lynched was his son. Kane obtained a court order for an exhumation, which took place on the 13th. When the body was brought up, Kane immediately recognized it by the missing finger as his son, Thomas J. Kane. Mr. Kane said his son had lost his finger while working as a railroad switchman and that he'd changed his name to Larkin after being blacklisted for participating in a railway strike. The father said Tom had always been a wayward son but had never previously committed any serious crimes to his knowledge. However, he said he had no hard feelings toward the people of Rhineland.

J. J. Kane had his son's body shipped back to New York for reburial.

Chapter Fifteen

They Want Me to Say Yes but They Can Kill Me Before I'll Do It
The Lynching of Henry Williams

After Henry Williams, a thirty-year-old black man, was arrested on the morning of June 29, 1898, at Macon, Missouri, for an attempted attack on a white girl the previous night and an alleged assault on two young white women a month earlier, he vehemently denied the crimes. "I am not that sort of man," he said. Speaking of the mob that was forming against him even as he spoke, he added, "They want me to say yes, but they can kill me before I'll do it."

And kill him is exactly what they did. Unmoved by Williams's protestations of innocence, they took him from jail late on the night of the 29th and hanged him from a railroad bridge at the edge of town. Macon's self-appointed dispensers of justice apparently gave more credence to the circumstantial evidence and to Williams's reputation for prior bad acts than they did to his denials.

On July 20, 1895, Williams had allegedly broken into Olga Horn's sleeping room above a music store in Macon at one o-clock in the morning and made a "desperate attempt to criminally assault her." The twenty-two-year-old Miss Horn identified Williams as her assailant, and he was arrested about the first of August and bound over to wait the action of a grand jury. Initially indicted for sexual assault, Williams pled not guilty. He changed his plea to guilty in early October when the charge was reduced to simple assault, "owing to the bad reputation" of Olga Horn and her sister, who was a prosecution witness in the case. Williams was sentenced to ninety days in jail and was given credit for the sixty days he'd already served.

About a year after Williams got out of jail upon completion of his sentence for assaulting Olga Horn, an outbreak of burglaries began in the Macon area. A lone thief started entering homes in the middle of the night, often residences where no men were present, and taking whatever articles of value he could find. At first, no one grew greatly alarmed, because no one got hurt.

But then about midnight on May 23, 1898, someone slipped into the home of Ann Browitt a mile west of Macon near the town's waterworks powerhouse and committed what the *Macon Republican* called "one of the most atrocious crimes that was ever perpetuated in the county." Ann's two oldest daughters, twenty-one-year-old Annie and eighteen-year-old Ethel, were asleep when they were startled by the sound of a bureau drawer opening and awoke to see a masked man standing in their downstairs bedroom holding a short-handled hoe. Terrified by the intrusion, one of the young women offered the man money or anything else they had on the premises, but he said that wasn't what he wanted.

The intruder then jumped onto the bed and struck Annie several times with the hoe. Ethel crawled out a low window to try to escape, but the villain chased her down and knocked her to the ground. He began to attack her, hitting her with the hoe and ripping her clothes off. Aroused by the commotion, Mrs. Browitt appeared on the scene with her twelve-year-old daughter and started to light a lamp. The assailant warned her not to, but she did so anyway, while Annie raced to a neighbor's house for help. Frightened either by the mother's lighting of the lantern or Annie's dash for help, the attacker suddenly jumped up, hopped over a fence, and disappeared into a nearby woods. The only clue as to the assailant's identity was that the twelve-year-old daughter said she saw the man lift his sleeve and scratch his arm when her mother lit the lantern and that his skin was black. That was enough to help get Henry Williams lynched when a similar attack occurred in Macon a month later.

On the late night of Tuesday, June 28, a man entered the home of John Koechel and went into the bedroom of Koechel's stepdaughters, fifteen-year-old Amelia Leubke and thirteen-year-old Ann Leubke. Grasping Amelia's arm when she awoke, the intruder threatened, "If you holler, I'll do you as I did the girls at the waterworks." At this point, an older stepdaughter, Bertha Leubke, heard the commotion from an adjoining room and appeared on the scene to frighten the man away.

As he was fleeing, the intruder grabbed a sack of flour from the Koechel residence and took it with him. Unbeknownst to the thief, the sack had a small leak in it, and after daylight the next morning, two local officers followed the trail of flour to the home of Henry Williams in the south part of Macon. Not only was the suspect bag of flour found at the residence but so, too, were a number of other articles, including a lot of ladies' apparel, that were identified as having been stolen from various Macon area homes. In addition, a bloody coat belonging to Williams was found in the home. It was thought to have been the coat worn by the assailant of the Browitt girls.

Over Williams's vehement protestations, both he and his wife were tossed in the Macon County Jail in Macon on Wednesday morning the 29th. The accused said he'd bought the flour from a local store and that he'd gotten the other suspect items found in his home from a traveling peddler. As for the coat, he said he got it from his father-in-law, who got it from another man, and if it had blood on it, he didn't know anything about it. The storekeeper confirmed that he'd sold Williams a sack of flour about a month earlier, but he added that Williams had recently come back to his store asking to buy another sack on credit and had been refused.

Nobody believed Williams's claims of innocence, and as word of his arrest spread throughout the morning of the

29th, people began gathering on the streets of Macon. They talked loosely about taking the law into their own hands, but there was no serious attempt to organize a lynch party.

On Wednesday afternoon, a *Macon Republican* reporter visited Williams in his cell. The prisoner prefaced the interview with a short summary of his life. He was born in Mississippi and got married in Memphis, but his first wife died. He then came to Missouri, where he married a second time in Marceline. After he separated from his second wife, he came to Macon and married Saphronia Nichols, and the couple had an infant child. Williams said he was a member of the Methodist church in Marceline but hadn't attended church regularly since he came to Macon.

The prisoner repeated his claim that he was not guilty of the crimes for which he'd been arrested. He said he went to a concert with his wife the previous evening and that, when it was over, they went straight home and went to bed. Williams also said he did not commit the attack a month earlier near the waterworks. He stressed that he did not say to Amelia Leubke, "If you holler, I will do you as I did the girls at the water works," because he did not commit either break-in. Nonetheless, those were the words that ended up costing Williams his life, according to the *Republican* reporter.

Addressing a rumor that had been circulating around Macon, Williams denied that he had killed a man during a fight at a coal mine in Alabama. He admitted that he'd worked in coal mines in Iowa and Missouri but not when he lived in the South, and he'd never even been to Alabama.

Returning to the most recent accusation against him, Williams swore that he did not break into the Koechel home the previous evening. "I positively deny that I have been to this house."

The first he knew about the break-in, he said, was when he went to a neighbor's place early this morning to do some chores and came back home to find the local officers there to arrest him.

Although the talk of lynching during the day "appeared to be more in a jocular way than serious," the mood of the people turned menacing after dark. Around ten o'clock small knots of men started forming around the courthouse, and they soon came together into one crowd and determined to carry out vigilante justice. A local minister made a speech imploring the mob to let the law take its course. He cited an instance he knew about in which a man who turned out to be innocent had been lynched. "He warmed to his subject and was making quite a talk,' observed the *Republican,* "but the crowd howled him down."

The mob then marched to the jail and demanded that Sheriff A. J. Glenn turn over the prisoner. Standing with two deputies in front of the jail at a fence that surrounded the building, Glenn refused, but his show of resistance failed to weaken the vigilantes' resolve. While they were contending with the sheriff, someone showed up with a rope, and the mob gave out a shout.

As the mood of the mob coarsened, a citizen named McVicker got up to speak, trying to get the crowd to disperse, but someone threw a rock at him and "knocked him senseless," said the *Macon Republican.* Sheriff Glenn, who was standing right beside McVicker, continued arguing with the crowd, assuring them that a full investigation of Williams's guilt would be undertaken the next day.

But the mob was in no mood for waiting. Some in the crowd knocked down the fence surrounding the jail, and some of the others joined in a rush toward the officers guarding the jail. Sheriff Glenn and his deputies were quickly disarmed, and the front door of the jail was battered in. The key to the jail corridor was located and the iron door unlocked. The would-be lynchers took Williams from his cell and herded him outside, where his appearance was greeted with wild hurrahs from the crowd.

The prisoner was taken a block north of the jail, where the leader of the mob stopped to interrogate him, supposedly giving Williams a chance to explain himself.

Described in contemporaneous newspapers only as "a tall man," the leader first asked the prisoner whether he had committed the crimes he was charged with, and Williams promptly denied having done so. The tall man then demanded to know where one of the articles of clothes found in Williams's house came from and where the blood on his coat came from, and the prisoner repeated the same explanations he'd given to the newspaperman earlier in the day.

Finally, the crowd started howling again, impatient to get on with the hanging bee. Rather than string the prisoner up on the spot, the mob decided to take him to the south edge of town and hang him to a Wabash Railroad bridge. Reversing direction, they marched Williams back through the streets of Macon. As the grim parade passed the jail, Williams asked to see his wife one last time so that he could bid her goodbye. Although most of the crowd seemed to oppose even this meager act of mercy, the tall leader consented. A runner hurried to the jail and quickly returned, reporting that the wife did not care to see her doomed husband.

The march continued south on Rollins Street to Weed and then west to the Wabash Road. Here Williams was positioned under the railroad bridge, where a little man in a white hat remarked, "Henry, …you are a brave man, and we're going to treat you right; if you want to say anything, now's your chance."

Williams declined the invitation to speak, but shortly afterward he asked the tall leader to tell his wife and child goodbye for him, and he once again asserted his innocence. The doomed man's hands and feet were bound, a noose was placed around his neck, and the other end was thrown up to a group of men on the bridge.

The men on the bridge started to pull, but the leader told them to wait. He asked Williams whether he'd prefer to be drawn up or to be taken onto the bridge and allowed to jump off. Williams told the tall man to suit himself, since he was the one doing the hanging.

Henry Williams, Hanged for Attempting an Assault on the Person of a 15=year= old girl.

Five Hundred People Took Part in the Lynching===Hanged From the Wabash Bridge in the Heart of the Ctity.

Headline from *La Plata Home Press* describing lynching of Williams.

The leader then bid the doomed man goodbye and signaled the men on the bridge to pull. They pulled, and Williams's body shot up. It was 12:30 a.m. on the 30th of June, 1898.

The men on the bridge pulled the body up high, let it down a ways, and then pulled it back up, but never letting it touch the ground. When the top end of the rope was finally tied fast to the bridge, a young man on the bridge started to sing a love song but, realizing the incongruity of it, abruptly stopped.

The lynch mob marched off into the night, leaving Williams's body dangling from the bridge. It was still hanging there after daylight on the morning of the 30th, "furnishing an uncanny spectacle for the passengers on the Hannibal and St. Joe Railroad trains," according to the *Republican*. Many curious citizens of Macon, also flocked to the scene to gaze at the suspended dead man. Several of the spectators were women whose homes had been broken into and who were drawn by a morbid desire to see the body of the man who'd allegedly committed the robberies.

The body was finally cut down about 8:30 a.m. and taken to the nearby railroad engine house, where Macon County coroner Guthrie Scrutchfield held an inquest. The jury reached the usual verdict in such cases, declaring that the deceased came to his death "at the hands of some two or three hundred men whose names, identities and residences are to these jurors unknown."

So, very little was ever done to try to bring the lynchers of Henry Williams to justice. This despite the fact that the identity of the tall leader of the mob was "pretty well known" in Macon, according to White's *General History of Macon County*, and he was still living in the community when the history was published twelve years after the lynching.

Chapter Sixteen

Quiet, Effective Work of the Benevolent Association
The Lynching of Benjamin Jones

On Saturday morning, September 10, 1898, Benjamin Jones, "a gray-haired man, sixty-eight years of age," who lived with his son in the Randolph area of Clay County, Missouri, volunteered to take his neighbors' eleven-year-old daughter, Annie Montgomery, to the county fair in Liberty about ten miles away. The girl's parents, James and Emma Montgomery, agreed to the arrangement, and Annie rode to Liberty with the old man in his big wagon.

During the morning, Jones took the girl shopping, and in the afternoon they went to the fair. As evening approached, the pair started back to Randolph, and during the return trip, the old codger sexually assaulted young Annie. Perhaps hoping the girl wouldn't tell, Jones continued the journey after the assault and delivered her to her home.

But Annie broke into tears upon entering the house and told her parents the whole story. James Montgomery immediately notified local constable David C. Roberts, who found Jones not far away, still on the road in his wagon. A posse of citizens who flocked to the scene talked of lynching the old man on the spot, but it was decided to let the officers deliver him to the county jail.

Jones was taken to Liberty and thrown in the clink on Sunday morning. As word of the previous day's assault spread, "the indignation of the Clay county people knew no bounds," according to the *Kansas City Journal*:

All day groups of men and boys could be seen standing around on the square and side streets, talking in low tones. Horses were hitched at every convenient hitching post. The male population had determined looks on their faces and anyone with an experienced eye could see that something was to happen to-night that would cause a sensation in the sleepy little town of Liberty on the following morning.

Despite the ominous mood in Liberty during the day, few people were on the streets Sunday night, and most of the citizens were "slumbering quietly in their beds" when the town's electric lights were suddenly extinguished shortly after eleven o'clock and "the sound of horses feet was soon heard clattering over the stony streets, leading to the square."

A masked mob of about a hundred men converged on the courthouse. They pounded open the jail door in short order, rushed in, and dragged Jones out, begging for his life and with a rope already around his neck. They took him to the front porch of the courthouse and tossed the other end of the rope over an overhead railing. The leader of the mob asked the old man whether he had anything to say. Jones admitted the deed but said he was drunk at the time, and he continued to plead for his life.

"Swing him up," the leader said, and the command was quickly obeyed.

Several hands pulled the doomed man up, and he swung out off the top step of the porch, suspended in the air. "There was a gurgling in his throat and movement of his legs for a few moments," said a report from Liberty that appeared in the *Mexico Weekly Ledger*, "but death was quick." Noting the same gurgling and convulsive shuddering, the *Kansas City Journal* added that a single gunshot also rang out, and then, "All was still."

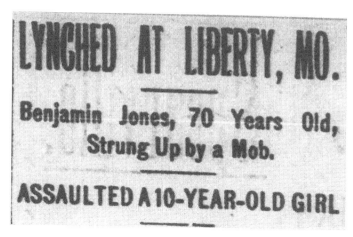

Headline describing lynching of Jones. *Dodge City Globe Republican.*

"Now go to your homes," ordered the gang leader, "and keep your mouths closed."

The lynchers soon dispersed, "as quietly as they had come," said the *Journal*. Jones's body was cut down and taken to a local undertaking firm. An examination revealed that Jones had been shot in the neck, which no doubt explains his quick death. The body was clad in a plain shirt with light pants and socks and no shoes.

According to the *Journal*, many of Liberty's citizens were surprised to learn of the lynching upon awaking the next morning, but they largely approved the extralegal proceeding, many of them "freely expressing admiration for the quiet, effective work of the benevolent association."

The dead man's son, Mit W. Jones, came to Liberty on Monday from his home at Randolph, but he refused to take charge of the body or even look at it. Mit and his brother, also a resident of Clay County, were said to be highly respected citizens, while the old man had been less well thought of, even before the incident that brought on the lynching. Benjamin Jones had supposedly served two years in the Missouri State Penitentiary for forgery, and he had recently been making a living as a quack druggist, traveling throughout Kansas and Oklahoma peddling potions of his own manufacture.

In the immediate wake of the attack on Annie Montgomery, physicians who examined her reportedly thought her injuries would prove fatal. They gave her only a one in ten chance of recovery. If this was true, the doctors were wrong. Two years later, at the time of the 1900 census, Annie was thirteen and still living with her parents in Clay County.

Chapter Seventeen

The Most Atrocious Crime in Dunklin County History
The Murder of the Tettaton Family

In December of 1900, after the Missouri Supreme Court upheld the murder conviction and death sentence of James H. Tettaton for killing his stepmother, his two half-brothers, and his two half-sisters in April of 1899 in Dunklin County, newspapers across the state applauded the decision, citing the brutality of the crime. The *St. Louis Republic*, for instance, said the "cruel and dastardly" multiple murder was "without a parallel" in the criminal history of Missouri.

Perhaps a slight exaggeration, but few people would dispute the more circumspect declaration of the *Moberly Weekly News* that the Tettaton crime was "the most atrocious in the history of Dunklin County."

About 9:00 p.m. on the night of April 25, 1899, neighbors of Jane Tettaton living about a mile and a quarter north of Malden were aroused by the sight of Mrs. Tettaton's home ablaze. Rushing to the scene, they found the home nearly consumed and the "sickening odor of burning flesh" rising from the pyre. Five bodies were dragged out of the fiery embers. They were burned almost beyond recognition, but they were identified by those intimately familiar with the age and size of each member of the family as Jane Tettaton and her four children: George, fifteen; Ben, eleven; Ida, nine; and Ada, seven.

Found lying in the yard not far from the burning house was James Henry Tettaton, stepson of Jane Tettaton and an older half-brother of her four children. The twenty-nine-year-old Tettaton had numerous knife wounds to his head and face, and he appeared to be unconscious. However, most people on the scene thought the wounds, which were superficial, were self-inflicted, because a bloody pocketknife belonging to Tettaton was found nearby, and most thought his blackout was a pretense. He was taken to a nearby house, where he soon revived enough to relate his story of what had happened.

He claimed the crime had been committed by two unknown men. He said he'd been talking to his stepmother shortly after eating supper with the family when the men entered the house with weapons drawn and demanded all the money he was carrying. When he refused, they started shooting and hit Jane at first fire. Tettaton said that he ran out of the house into the yard, where he was cut and beat into unconsciousness, and that he was unaware of what happened after that.

Tettaton had previously borne a good reputation and was on the board of trustees for the village of Bernie, eight miles north of Malden in Stoddard County. Few people believed his tale, though, because he "told many conflicting stories about the affair" and he was known to have previously been at odds with his stepmother over his father's estate.

The father, Washington Tettaton, was a well-to-do farmer whose first wife, James's mother, died when James was four years old. Wash remarried Malinda Jane Smith in 1881, when she was in her early twenties and James was not quite twelve years old. After Wash died near the beginning of 1897, James was named administrator of his father's estate, and a dispute developed between James and Jane over his apportioning of the estate. She filed a petition in probate court for admeasurement of the homestead upon which she and Wash were living at the time of his death. She also sued James in circuit court and won a settlement of $500.

Sketch of James Tettaton from *St. Louis Post-Dispatch.*

One of the conflicting stories James Tettaton told after the murders were discovered concerned a bloody note found near the spot where he was lying. Tettaton said he went to Jane's house on the evening of the 25th to pay off the remainder of the $500 settlement, but the note, signed by Jane Tettaton and acknowledging receipt of $350, was dated a month earlier. Tettaton explained the discrepancy by saying that he'd gone to Jane's house in March to pay the $350 and counted out the money, that she'd handed him the receipt at that time, but that a dispute had then developed about interest on the debt and he kept the money and forgot to return the receipt. In any case, the receipt was thought to be a counterfeit.

Another inconsistency in Tettaton's story concerned a pistol found in the debris of the burned house, which, Tettaton acknowledged, belonged to him. He said he'd laid it on a bed in the house earlier in the evening but had removed the cartridges before doing so in order that the children wouldn't find it and hurt themselves with it. Yet the cartridges were not in his vest pocket where he said he'd put them, but instead a number of spent cartridge shells that matched the caliber of the pistol were found in the debris.

In addition, a neighbor girl of Mrs. Tettaton told of a conversation she'd had with Jane on the day before she died during which Jane said she feared something might happen to her. The neighbor's mother also said that James Tettaton had recently paid a mysterious visit to Jane's home late at night during which he lit a match outside a window but did not announce his visit or ask admittance.

Tettaton was arrested on suspicion on the night of the murders and held temporarily at Malden. A coroner's jury convened the next day and concluded beyond question that George Tettaton, the oldest boy, came to his death by reason of a bullet through the head. The evidence showed that one other child had also been shot, while the mother and the other two kids had been clubbed to death, prior to the house being burned. Three jurymen urged a verdict charging Tettaton with the murders, but three others wanted to interview the suspect before concluding that he was the murderer. However, he had already been whisked away from Dunklin County for safekeeping before the inquest ended, and the inquiry therefore adjourned without a verdict.

The three cautious jurors were in the minority, though, because most folks considered the overwhelming circumstantial evidence all the proof they needed. Because of the intense feeling against the suspect, the Malden city marshal and the Dunklin County sheriff escorted him to Cairo, Illinois, on April 27 with the intention of taking him to St. Louis for safekeeping. Instead, he was taken back across the river to Missouri and finally jailed at Jackson, the seat of Cape Girardeau County.

The lack of unanimity at the coroner's inquest held no sway over the grand jury either. The last week of May, Tettaton was brought to the Dunklin County seat at Kennett and indicted on five separate charges of first-degree murder. Afterward, he was held in the Dunklin County Jail.

Prosecutors elected to try Tettaton first on the charge of murdering his half-brother George, because the identity of the victim and the evidence of his death by gunfire prior to the house-burning were the clearest in his case. The trial was held during the October term of Dunklin County Circuit Court. On November 3, the jury returned a verdict of guilty, and the next day Judge James L. Fort sentenced Tettaton to hang on December 15, 1899. The defense's immediate appeal to the Missouri Supreme Court, however, acted as a stay of execution.

On the morning of January 6, 1890, Tettaton and another convicted killer, Milo Gregory, escaped from the Dunklin County Jail by tunneling under their cells. Dunklin County sheriff William R. Satterfield offered a reward of $200 each for their recapture, and on January 8 Missouri governor Lon Stephens added a state reward of $300 each. The fugitives were caught on January 15 near Neeleyville in Butler County and lodged in jail at Poplar Bluff overnight. The next day they were returned to the Dunklin County Jail at Kennett.

A few months later, Sheriff Satterfield, fearing another jailbreak or a lynching, escorted Tettaton and Gregory to St. Louis for safekeeping. Interviewed by a *Post-Dispatch* reporter about the first of July at the city jail, Tettaton denied his guilt and expressed hope that the high court would give him another chance to prove his innocence. The story he told the newspaperman was similar to what he'd said when first arrested. He claimed he was in the house with Jane and her kids when someone shot the woman through a window, but beyond that he could only speculate because he himself was knocked unconsciousness by a blow from the butt of a gun. He managed to drag himself outside but did not know what happened after that. The reporter did not ask the obvious question: *Why would the assailants want to kill a mother and her four young children but only conk him in the head?* And Tettaton did not volunteer such information.

The St. Louis newspaperman described Tettaton as "a big and powerful man, six feet tall" and weighing about 200 pounds. "He is red-faced, freckled, has a shock of rough brown hair and a long red mustache. He wears the clothing of one of the poorer classes of southeast Missouri farmers."

The Missouri Supreme Court took up Tettaton's case at the October 1900 term. The justices rejected several defense arguments relating to legalities, such as a claim that Tettaton should have been granted a change of venue, and they found that the evidence and "criminating circumstances" showed beyond a reasonable doubt that "George Tettaton was shot and killed, and point(ed) as conclusively and unerringly to the guilt of the defendant as does the needle to the pole." The high court thus affirmed the lower court's verdict and reset the execution for January 25, 1901.

Tettaton's and Gregory's lawyers appealed to incoming Missouri governor Alexander M. Dockery, and the new governor's first official act, on January 14, was to grant stays of execution to both men so that he might consider their cases. Tettaton's hanging was rescheduled for February 19, pending the governor's final decision. A few days after granting the stays, Dockery announced that he would not further interfere in either case. Speaking of the Tettaton case, the governor called the multiple murder "one of the most terrible crimes in the history of the state." While allowing that the evidence was largely circumstantial, he said it "abundantly justified the verdict of the jury and has received the approval of the both the circuit and supreme courts. A defenseless woman and her four children were murdered and then burned. The facts all point to the defendant as their murderer, and I shall not disturb the verdict."

Tettaton vowed not to die on the gallows, and on the evening of February 16, just three days before his scheduled execution, he attempted suicide by cutting his wrist with a piece of broken mirror. Milo Gregory, who was his cellmate, saw him slice his wrist but declined to alert anyone. Instead, he simply watched as Tettaton lay bleeding to death.

The dying man was discovered "very weak and almost unconscious" by the jailer during a routine cell check. Stationing a deputy at the cell door as a guard, the jailer partially staunched the bleeding by wrapping a handkerchief around Tettaton's wrist. A doctor was promptly summoned, and he stopped the flow of blood and bandaged the wound. When Tettaton regained full consciousness, he "seemed greatly chagrined" that his attempt to kill himself had failed, and a close guard was placed over him to prevent him from re-opening the wound.

About 1:30 in the afternoon of February 19, Tettaton, accompanied by his spiritual adviser, was led to the scaffold by the sheriff and several deputies. A small door in the stockade was opened so that Tettaton might address the large crowd outside. He spoke for about fifteen minutes, admitting that he had instigated the murders but insisting that he had hired two men, W. T. Barham and A. J. Ransom, to carry them out. He said he paid them $500.

After the condemned man's speech, the door was closed and the final preparations were made. A black cap was placed over his head and a noose adjusted around his neck. The sheriff pulled a lever dropping Tettaton through the trap at 2:10 p.m. in front of about 100 spectators who'd been allowed on the platform. He was declared dead and the body cut down after nineteen minutes. The body was placed in a coffin and turned over to friends, who took it back to Bernie for burial beside Tettaton's first wife, who had died in 1897.

Chapter Eighteen

A Tragedy of the Tenderloin District
The Murder of Pearl Clark and Hanging of Steve Clark

Reporting on the October 1901 trial of Steve Clark for the murder of his common-law wife, Pearl Clark, at Poplar Bluff, Missouri, a few months earlier, the *Poplar Bluff Republican* called the crime "a tragedy of the 'Tenderloin District'" because the "star actors," the victim and the murderer, belonged to two classes known as the courtesan and the gambler.

But to call Pearl Clark a "courtesan" and Steve Clark a "gambler" without also appending the title "pimp" to his name elevated them from the underbelly of society to a plane of respectability they never enjoyed. Poplar Bluff didn't have courtesans. It had women "of bad reputation." It had "degraded women." It might even have had prostitutes. But it didn't have "courtesans." And its "tenderloin district" was hardly large enough to justify the word "district."

During the previous spring, twenty-six-year-old Pearl, according to the *Poplar Bluff Daily Republican*, had "conducted a house of prostitution in a two-story yellow frame house in the southeast corner of the city." Citizens of Poplar Bluff called the place the "Rabbit House."

Pearl, whose maiden name was Alice Bryan, had been married twice, once to a man named Giles. Some reports gave her name as Alice Giles, but she went by Pearl Clark, because she had taken in professional gambler Steve Clark as her lover and common-law husband.

The thirty-five-year-old Clark "encouraged her loathsome profession by pimping for her resort, and thus did his share to assist her in her nefarious vocation" so he could avoid having to work for a living. Pearl's calling required her "to look and act sweet on all men," and Clark accepted her flirtations as simply a part of business until Ed Lewis appeared on the scene and a "green-eyed monster" reared its head. A brakeman on the Iron Mountain Railroad, Lewis started spending too much time with Pearl to suit Steve Clark and "the smiles and glances became too serious."

Clark and Pearl quarreled over the matter several times. Finally Clark told her not to have anything more to do with Lewis, and Pearl promised to quit seeing the other man. Her tempestuous relationship with Clark calmed, and they sailed along smoothly for a few weeks.

But then on June 25, 1901, Clark found Lewis and Pearl talking together near the Iron Mountain depot in Poplar Bluff. Accosting them in anger, Clark scolded Pearl for not keeping her word and warned Lewis to leave Pearl alone. Pearl finally got Clark to calm down and return home with her, promising once again to be true to him. Back at the house, Clark warned Pearl that if she didn't keep her word this time, he would kill her.

"But a prostitute's word is no better than her morals," said the *Daily Republican.* Later that same day, Pearl went to a wine room at a saloon in the south end of Poplar Bluff with a friend, Maggie Dawson, and they met Lewis there. (Saloons were strictly male domains in 1901, but so-called "wine rooms," where women and dancing were allowed, were sometimes attached to saloons. Women who frequented such joints were shunned by polite society.)

In the late afternoon, Clark found Lewis and Pearl together at the wine room and immediately flew into a rage. Confronting Lewis, he grabbed a large iron cuspidor and raised it over his head as if to strike the other man, but Lewis suddenly pulled out a revolver and forced Clark to back off.

Clark left in angry humiliation and went downtown to try to borrow a gun from one of his acquaintances. Failing this, he returned to the Rabbit House, secured a big butcher knife, and went back to town to sharpen it.

In the meantime, Pearl, realizing how distraught Clark was, left Lewis soon after the altercation at the wine room and returned home with Maggie. About 6:00 p.m., Pearl and another woman were standing on the back porch and Maggie and her male companion, Ed Bowen, were lying in a hammock stretched between the porch and a nearby tree. Another man, Jake Kern, was also present. One of the five noticed Clark approaching on the street in front of the house and said, "Here comes Steve."

Moments later, Clark walked through the house, came onto the back porch, and went straight to Pearl, who was standing with a dipper of water in one hand and a newspaper in the other. Grasping her by the arm, Clark said, "Pearl, I told you I would kill you if you ever went with Lewis again. Now, I have to kill you, then I am going to kill myself."

Laughing off the threat, Pearl asked, "Don't you want to kiss me goodbye? Steve, you are not going to kill me. You would not kill anyone. Go away and behave yourself."

Pearl's flippant manner only excited Steve's fury the more. Pulling the knife from his waistband, he struck her with it, cutting her hands first and then stabbing her in the side in the area of the heart.

"Oh, Ed, you are not going let him kill me, are you?" Pearl appealed to Bowen as she collapsed.

"But Bowen thought that safety lay in flight" and took off, according to the *Daily Republican*. Maggie lingered just a few moments longer before she, too, fled the scene.

After the witnesses were gone and Pearl lay dead or dying, Steve stabbed himself in the chest just above the heart and lay down to die beside his victim. Poplar Bluff police chief John Harding arrived on the scene shortly afterwards and found Pearl lying dead in a pool of blood. Not far from her body her murderer lay moaning and praying for God to let him die. He said that he had killed Pearl, that he couldn't live without her, and that he wanted to be buried with her.

But Clark's wound was not fatal or even life-threatening. Harding arrested him and took him to the county jail, where his wound was dressed. A murder charge was filed against Clark, and he was soon well enough to answer the charge. Clark pleaded not guilty at his arraignment and was bound over for trial at the October term of the Butler County Circuit Court.

Clark testified in his own defense at the trial on October 18. He freely admitted stabbing Pearl but said he acted out of passion in the heat of the moment. After relating his previous encounters with Ed Lewis and his jealousy of the relationship between Lewis and Pearl, Clark said that, on the day of the crime, he heard a male voice in the backyard as he approached the house and thought it belonged to Lewis. Passing through the house, he picked up a butcher knife in the dining room and stabbed Pearl in a fit of anger after she hit him first when he confronted her.

Maggie Dawson and Ed Bowen were the principal witnesses for the prosecution. Refuting the defense's contention that Clark acted out of passion on the spur of the moment, Maggie said that Clark did not retrieve the butcher knife as he passed through the house just prior to the crime because it was already missing when she and Pearl came home. Both Maggie and Bowen denied that Pearl had struck Clark first, and even Jake Kern, who testified for the defense, agreed Pearl had not hit Clark first.

Testimony concluded on the night of the 18th, and the jury came back with a verdict the next morning finding Clark guilty of murder in the first degree. A few days later, at the end of the October term, Judge James L. Fort sentenced Clark to hang on December 10. The case, however, was appealed to the Missouri Supreme Court, and the execution was postponed pending the outcome of the appeal.

Steve Clark from the *St. Louis Post-Dispatch.*

When the high court finally took up the case a year later, at the October 1902 term, the justices concluded that "under the evidence defendant was clearly and manifestly guilty of murder in the first degree." They added that the "homicide was of the most brutal character, and without cause or excuse." On November 18, the judgment of the lower court was affirmed, and Clark's execution date was reset for December 19, 1902.

On December 17, two days before Clark was scheduled to die, Missouri governor A. M. Dockery granted him a reprieve, postponing the execution date until January 16, 1903. A few weeks later, Dockery intervened again. Will Gatlin, a black man, was scheduled to hang in Poplar Bluff on February 6 for his part in the murder of another black man three months after Pearl Clark's murder, and the townspeople petitioned Dockery that Clark's execution be postponed again so that both men could hang on the same day. The governor granted the request on January 6.

When a local reporter called at the Butler County Jail to visit the condemned men on February 4, he found Clark seemingly "in good spirits and not the least downhearted," although he was unwilling to talk for publication. Gatlin, on the other hand, was "rather dejected."

Clark's short march to the scaffold just outside the Butler County Jail began at 1:55 p.m. February 6. He made a brief final statement, admitting he'd committed a terrible act during a fit of jealousy but declaring himself not guilty of first degree murder. Then, the black cap was adjusted and the other preparations were made very quickly. Clark was dropped through the trap at exactly 2:00 p.m. and was pronounced dead fifteen minutes later. The body was cut down at 2:23 and placed in a coffin for burial at the city cemetery, as he'd requested, beside the woman he'd killed.

Gatlin mounted the scaffold soon after Clark's body was removed. In contrast to Clark, Gatlin delayed his hanging by talking, praying, and preaching for over a half hour before he was finally launched into the hereafter at 3:14 p.m.

Chapter Nineteen

A Sunday Lynching at Paris
The Vigilante Hanging of Abraham Witherup

After the body of William Grow was found floating in the North Fork of the Salt River in northeastern Monroe County, Missouri, on April 22, 1902, five days after he'd gone missing, Abraham Witherup, who'd been living with the victim on a nearby farm for the past few months, was immediately suspected of murdering him. Witherup denied any knowledge of the crime when he was arrested on the 23rd, but he confessed the next day, claiming he'd killed Grow only after the young man had attacked him. His failure to report Grow's death immediately and his efforts instead to cover it up undermined his plea of self-defense, of course, but it's not at all clear that a more timely confession would have made much difference to Grow's father and the rest of the angry mob that ended up lynching Witherup.

A native of Ohio, the fifty-five-year-old Witherup, was a "tall, raw-boned man with a short, stubby, blonde beard," according to the *St. Louis Post-Dispatch*. He weighed about 180 pounds, and his blue eyes were described as "evasive and restless." Witherup had lived in Kansas during the latter part of the nineteenth century, but he landed in Missouri prior to 1900. Divorced from his first wife, he married Mary A. Miller in Monroe County in April of 1899, but the second marriage didn't last either, ending in divorce within a year.

Near the beginning of 1902, twenty-two-year-old William Grow, a native of Monroe County, rented sixty acres of land from Mrs. Henry Johnson a few miles south of Hunnewell. In February, he invited Witherup to move onto the land with him and share the crop they raised in exchange for Witherup paying part of the rent. When Witherup moved onto the property, Grow told him, according to Witherup's later story, that he had an oral agreement with Mrs. Johnson but no written contract.

On Sunday, April 13, William Grow paid a visit to the home of his parents, Stephen and Mary Belle Grow, near Paris. He left the next day wearing a gold watch and a gold ring and carrying seven dollars in his pocketbook. He reached the Johnson farm safely, as one or more neighbors saw him a couple of days after he got back, but nobody saw him after April 17. No one thought anything about it, however, because the Johnson property sat a quarter of a mile off the road in a secluded area, and Grow and Witherup had only occasional contact with the outside world.

Then, on Monday, April 21, Witherup showed up at the Stephen Grow place to ask Grow whether he or his wife had seen anything out of their son. Witherup said the young man had left the Johnson farm the previous Thursday evening and had not come back. Concerned, the Grows sent word to surrounding neighbors to be on the lookout for their missing son.

The next afternoon, April 22, two men were fishing on the North Fork of the Salt River near Clinton School at a place called Paint Bank when they spied a strange object floating in midstream. Investigating, they found it to be a human body. They didn't recognize it as William Grow, but aware of the young man's disappearance, they sent for Stephen Grow.

Grow hurried to the scene and immediately identified the body of his son, although the head and face had been terribly mutilated. It appeared the young man had been foully murdered. One eye had been knocked in, and there were seven wounds about the head, any one of which could have been fatal. Word of the apparent crime was sent immediately to the county seat at Paris, and early the next morning, April 23, the acting coroner and other officials, including Prosecuting Attorney Frank McAllister and Sheriff James W. Clark, came to the scene. The coroner conducted an inquest and concluded that William Grow had come to his death at the hands of an unknown murderer.

After the inquest, Stephen Grow accompanied the officials three miles from the river to the home where his son had been living, and they found that parts of the floor had been freshly painted with red paint. A broom and an old rocking chair were also smeared with red paint. However, bloodstains were visible beneath the paint, and when a part of the floor was taken up, splotches of blood were clearly visible on the rocks beneath.

The investigators examined Witherup's wagon and found that the wood had been chiseled off in places, but spots of blood were still visible on the running gear. Having examined William's body and his belongings inside the house, Stephen Grow concluded that his son's gold ring and gold watch were missing, as was an almost new pair of pants he owned. The body, when found, had been dressed partly in Sunday clothes and partly in everyday clothes, with his shoes unlaced, as if someone had taken off part of his garments and haphazardly dressed him in different clothes. And a pile of ashes from a recent fire was found near the house, as if someone had burned the discarded clothes and other items to try to dispose of evidence.

Leaving the Johnson place, Stephen Grow took the county officials to his own home, where they discovered Abe Witherup sitting at the dinner table partaking of a meal Mrs. Grow had prepared. Witherup had paid another call to ask the Grows again whether they had seen their son recently, but now that the young man's body had been found, with all evidence pointing to Witherup as the killer, he was taken into custody at once.

Witherup feigned surprise as Clark put the handcuffs on him and told him he was under arrest on suspicion of having killed William Grow. The suspect claimed he knew nothing of young Grow except that he left the Johnson place the previous Thursday evening, April 17, saying he was going to a neighbor's house, and hadn't come back. Witherup said he and William Grow had never had any difficulty. He gave no particular reason for having painted the floors red, but he acknowledged that he did so, admitting that he'd traveled to Hunnewell on Friday to buy oil for mixing the paint and had painted the floors upon his return.

Arrested and taken to the Monroe County Jail in Paris, Witherup was examined and found to have blood on his underwear. The next day, April 24, he made a full confession, first to his spiritual advisor and then in a written statement to Prosecutor McAllister. He admitted to killing William Grow but claimed he did so in self-defense.

According to Witherup's story, the two men got into a dispute on the morning of April 17 over the rent payment. Grow told Witherup he had a written contract with Mrs. Johnson and that Witherup's name was not on the contract, intimating that he could have Witherup put off the land if he chose to do so. Witherup called Grow a liar, reminding him that he'd said back in February he had no written agreement. Witherup told Grow he'd either lied when the two first made their bargain or he was lying now.

The argument died down, but it flared back up that evening when Witherup declined to accompany Grow on a visit to a neighbor's house as Grow proposed. The quarrel quickly returned to the subject of the morning squabble, and Witherup again accused Grow of having lied one time or the other.

According to Witherup, Grow, in response to the accusation, grabbed a rocking chair and struck the older man a slight blow on the shoulder with it and then hit him again on the leg. Witherup grabbed a nearby hatchet and hit Grow with it. Staggered but still on his feet, Grow came at Witherup with the chair again, and Witherup struck the younger man with the hatchet a second time, knocking him to the floor, where he lay lifeless.

That same night, Witherup loaded Grow's body into his wagon with a little hay thrown over it and hauled it to the river, where he dumped it. The next morning, he traveled to town to buy oil for mixing the paint and spent the rest of the day on Friday the 18th painting everything red.

Almost nobody believed Witherup's claim of self-defense. Not only did his attempt to cover up the crime belie his claim, but his story contained inconsistencies and did not adequately account for the evidence. For instance, he claimed that he hit Grow with the hatchet only twice, but the evidence showed the victim had been struck multiple times. Grow's watch and ring were not found, but Witherup said he knew nothing about them. The pocketbook was found minus the seven dollars, but Witherup said he also knew nothing about the missing money. In addition, he could not say why Grow was dressed partly in Sunday clothes and partly in old work clothes with his shoes unlaced, because he claimed he carried the young man to the river in the same condition in which he was killed. Finally, Witherup said the death struggle occurred in the southwest corner of the room, but much of the blood was in the northeast corner, where the bed on which Grow slept was located. This led Prosecutor McAllister to theorize that Witherup had attacked his victim as he slept or prepared for sleep and then haphazardly dressed him after he killed him.

After Witherup's arrest and confession, stories began to circulate painting the prisoner as a heinous villain. One report claimed Witherup was "a study for criminologists" with "a ferocious and bloody bent of...mind" The story continued, "It has been known to the local authorities for several years that Witherup was suspected of killing a boy near Medicine Lodge, Kansas under almost identical circumstances" as the Grow murder, although evidence was never sufficient to arrest him. After Witherup's arrest, word leaked that Mrs. Miller, his second wife, had supposedly stated that Witherup admitted the Kansas crime to her. In addition, she said her ex-husband "would go into insane rages at his horses and come for his gun to kill them."

Witherup asked James H. Whitecotton, former Speaker of the House in the Missouri Legislature, to represent him, but Whitecotton refused. The prisoner finally retained Claud E. Snell as his lawyer.

The defendant was scheduled for arraignment on Saturday, May 24, a month after his arrest, and a rumor developed that a mob might try to take him from the officers as he was being led from the jail to the courtroom; so officials held the arraignment early that morning before many people were in town and prior to the originally scheduled time. At the arraignment, Judge David Eby set Witherup's trial date for June 30.

The premature arraignment and the judge's setting of a not-so-prompt trial date were said to have incited the would-be vigilantes even more. They wanted to see Witherup punished, and they didn't want to wait yet another month.

Men, most of them from north of Paris in the area where the crime had occurred, came into town throughout the day and evening on Saturday until "by 11:00 o'clock the streets were thronged," according to the *St. Louis Republic*, "and it was plain to be seen" that the mob, led by Stephen Grow, "meant to get Witherup, even if they should have to tear down the jail to do so."

Sheriff Clark and his deputies secured the jail early in the evening, and Grow went to the sheriff to demand that the keys be turned over to him and his cohorts. The sheriff refused, and he and his deputies, posted outside the door with drawn revolvers, held off the crowd for several hours.

In the meantime, a number of citizens went to Grow and his allies and implored them to abandon their attempt to take the law into their own hands. The crowd dispersed, and it was thought they'd gone home. Instead, they'd merely moved to the east part of town to plot an assault on the jail.

After midnight on Sunday morning, nine men went to a local blacksmith shop and secured sledgehammers and iron bars with which to break open the jail. They marched toward the jail and were commanded to halt when they were within a few paces. Instead of obeying the order, they rushed toward the jail, overpowered the officers, and disarmed them. Sheriff Clark and one of his deputies were slightly injured in the scuffle.

Several men stood guard over the officers, while the others attacked the outer door with sledgehammers. It yielded quickly to the blows, and it also did not take long for the mob to force an entrance to Witherup's cell. The gang had just placed a rope around the prisoner's neck when Whitecotton pushed his way through the mob to confront the leaders. He pleaded with them, for the sake of themselves and their families and for the sake of justice and the good name of Monroe County, to desist their unlawful action. Reminding them that he had refused to represent Witherup, he told them that he would also refuse to represent them and would instead assist in their prosecution.

His pleas and words of warning, however, did not deter the enraged crowd. The mob swept past Whitecotton and the officers, herding Witherup along with them, out into the street with a rope around his neck. The vigilantes took their prisoner up Main Street about a quarter of a mile to the Palmyra Bridge, an iron structure spanning the Middle Fork of the Salt River at the north edge of town.

Given a chance to speak or say a final prayer, Witherup said he had nothing further to say or confess beyond what he'd already offered, and he said he'd done all the praying he wanted to do while he was in his cell. When Stephen Grow asked specific questions about the killing of his son, Witherup repeated the story he'd already told, saying that he'd killed William Grow in self-defense, that he wasn't sure how many times he'd struck him, and that he didn't know what became of the young man's watch and money. He also denied the report that he had killed a boy in Kansas.

"Witherup was the most composed man in the crowd," according to a report in the *St. Louis Republic*, "and talked as quietly and rationally as though he was speaking in private conversation. He was not nervous or excited in the least, did not beg or plead for anything whatever but met death bravely and without evidence of fear."

Abe Witherup from the *St. Louis Republic*.

After Witherup finished answering the questions put to him, his feet were bound together and his hands tied behind his back. Ordered to get up on the railing of the bridge and jump off, he said he couldn't do so with his feet tied; so he was picked up by several men and placed on the railing in a sitting position. He sat there for a moment with nobody making a move. At exactly 2:00 a.m. on Sunday morning, May 25, 1902, Stephen Grow gave him a push that "sent him far out into the air and into eternity."

At 8:00 a.m. the county coroner summoned a jury, and the party went out to the scene, cut the body down, and brought it back to the courthouse in Paris. The body was embalmed, and an inquest scheduled for Tuesday the 27th. Although Prosecutor McAllister announced prior to the inquest that he knew the names of the men who took the most active part in the lynching and intended to prosecute to the full extent of the law, the coroner's jury reached the usual, innocuous verdict that the deceased had come to his death at the hands of parties unknown.

The lynching itself and the failure of Monroe County authorities to aggressively prosecute the mob was the subject of widespread criticism from surrounding counties. The *Shelbina Democrat* editor O. L. Jewett, for example, declared that the lynching of Witherup was "a greater crime than that of the aged prisoner." Jewett especially blamed Sheriff Clark and his deputies for not putting up a stronger defense against the mob. On the other hand, the local press, including the *Paris Mercury* and the *Monroe City Democrat*, strongly defended the vigilante action and said that for Sheriff Clark to have resorted to gunplay in order to stop the mob would have been foolhardy, because protecting the scoundrel Witherup was not worth the likely injuries and loss of other lives that would have resulted.

On June 30, the date originally set for Witherup's trial, Judge Eby came to Paris and called a grand jury for the purpose of investigating the mob action against the now-deceased defendant. Meeting on July 3, the jury failed to indict any of the mob, reportedly voting eight in favor of indictment and four against, which fell one vote short of the necessary three-fourths majority.

Chapter Twenty

A Black and White Lynching
Two Chicken Thieves Strung Up

After prominent Lafayette County farmer George W. Johnson was killed in the wee hours of August 5, 1902, when he interrupted two chicken thieves on his farm south of Lexington, Charles Salyers and Harry Gates were arrested on suspicion later the same morning. Fearing mob violence, Lafayette County sheriff Oscar Thomas tried to move the prisoners to Kansas City that afternoon, but he and his posse got only as far as Myrick, a couple of miles west of Lexington, before they were overtaken by several hundred men demanding that the suspects be brought back to Lexington. The gang assured the sheriff that they would do the prisoners no harm if they were brought back. Thomas let himself be persuaded, and both parties turned around and went back to Lexington together.

Rumors of vigilantism continued to swirl for the next day or two, but by August 9, things had settled down to the point that the editor of the *Lexington Intelligencer* was convinced that the law would be allowed to take its course. "The prisoners are as safe from mob violence," opined the newspaperman, "as they would be in the catacombs of Paris."

Well, not quite, as it turned out.

Both Gates, who was black, and Salyers, who was white, gave confessions after they were brought back to Lexington from Myrick, and their stories largely agreed as far as their movements leading up to the killing of George Johnson. The two men had gotten together in Lexington on the night of August 4 to shoot craps, and when they parted that evening, they agreed to meet back up a few hours later near Johnson's place to steal some of his chickens. They sneaked into Johnson's henhouse shortly after 2:00 a.m. and loaded more than a dozen chickens each into two gunny sacks. They had just made their escape through a fence when Johnson, alerted by an electric alarm system he'd recently installed in his henhouse, confronted them on the road that ran in front of his house.

Both men agreed that Johnson fired two shots at them when they failed to respond promptly to his order to halt and that one of the shots slightly wounded Gates.

But what the thirty-one-year-old Gates and twenty-three-year-old Salyers couldn't agree on was whose idea it was to steal the chickens in the first place and who had fired the fatal shots at Johnson. Each one blamed the other on both counts.

Salyers claimed at first that neither he nor Gates had a weapon when they went to the Johnson place but that, after Johnson fired at them with a pistol, Gates wrested it away from Johnson and shot him with it. Gates, who'd previously served a three-year term in the state penitentiary for second degree burglary, countered that Johnson fired at them with a shotgun and that Salyers returned fire with a pistol he had brought with him, killing Johnson. Gates said he didn't even know his partner in crime had a weapon until he heard Salyers fire the shots that killed Johnson as he (Gates) was running away.

Salyers's initial claim that Johnson had fired at him and Gates with a pistol cast doubt on his story, because the evidence showed that Johnson had used a shotgun, as Gates said. Salyers finally admitted the pistol that killed Johnson belonged to him, but he claimed he'd given it to Gates on the night of August 4. Still, few people believed Salyers's story. "The statement made by Salyers is incorrect," declared the *Lexington News*, "as it is definitely known by the officers that he fired the shot that killed Mr. Johnson."

Gates's lesser culpability, however, didn't seem to matter to the would-be lynchers of Lafayette County. He was a black chicken thief, and George Johnson was dead. That was good enough for them.

In the wee hours of August 12, exactly a week after Johnson's death, a mob of about 200 masked men swarmed into Lexington from the south, shut off electricity to the downtown area, and surrounded the courthouse square. On foot except for two surreys they'd brought along in which to convey the prisoners, the vigilantes knocked down the wooden west door of the jail and overpowered Sheriff Thomas and his deputies. They demanded that both prisoners be turned over to them, but Thomas refused. The would-be lynchers next demanded the keys to the cell, but the sheriff refused that order as well.

The "captain" of the gang then ordered his followers to cut open the cell doors, and one man, stepping forward with a hammer and chisel, went to work on the steel door of the cell holding Charles Salyers. Seemingly unruffled by the menacing racket, Salyers awoke and calmly rolled and lit a cigarette as the pounding continued. Breaking open the cell "was a hard job," said the *Lexington News*, "and the blows of the hammer could be heard several blocks away. It took fifteen minutes to cut the bolts, and the door swung open."

Salyers was pulled from his upstairs cell, and three men took him downstairs and outside onto the courthouse yard. The commotion had attracted a large crowd of curious onlookers, but masked sentinels placed around the courtyard ordered the people to stay on the north side of Main Street.

Meanwhile, other members of the gang went to work on Gates's downstairs cell door, which yielded to the hammer in only ten minutes. Gates was herded outside to join his fellow prisoner, and the leader of the mob gave an order to move out. It was not quite 2:00 a.m.

Harry Gates and Charles Salyers from the *St. Louis Republic*.

Loading their captives aboard the surreys, the vigilantes formed south of the courthouse on Franklin Street, tramped east to Twelfth Street, and then south, merging onto the old Columbus road (present-day Business 13). At the Tevis Bridge on the south edge of town, they reclaimed their horses and rode south about two and half miles to Edenview Church, not far from the scene of the week-old crime.

The prisoners were positioned beneath an elm tree in the northeast corner of the churchyard, where they were given a chance to say any last words they might wish to offer. Both men clung to their previous statements accusing the other of killing George Johnson. The contradicting statements caused an argument between the condemned men, with Gates demanding of Salyers why he would want to die "with a lie on his lips." Gates's statement was "more consistent," according to the *Lexington Intelligencer*, but his apparent honesty bought him no mercy.

Both men were swung up simultaneously to the same limb of the elm tree and left "hanging between heaven and earth," as the mob dispersed. About 4:00 a.m. the same morning, county officers went out the scene of the lynching, cut the bodies down, and brought them back to Lexington.

Salyers's body was turned over to his family, while Gates was buried at county expense, and it's not clear whether an inquest was even held before the interments.

The last official word on the lynching was apparently Lafayette County prosecuting attorney Horace F. Blackwell's statement to the press a day or two later that he had recognized many in the mob, that some of them were his best friends in the county, and that it was "premature to state now whether he would take any official action as to the mob's work."

Blackwell was far from the only one who seemed content to let the mob action stand without further inquiry. The editor of the *Lexington Intelligencer* seemed to reflect the view of many local citizens when, speaking of the lynching, he stated, "Prosecuting Attorney Blackwell, Sheriff Thomas and Deputy Kincaid have done everything in their power since the first to avoid this trouble.... Further resistance would have been foolhardy."

Lafayette County in general and Sheriff Thomas in particular were not, however, without their critics, especially from outside the county. A correspondent to the *Kansas City Star*, for instance, chastised both the citizens of Lexington for taking the lynching in stride and Sheriff Thomas for not doing more to prevent it. The writer lamented that the lynching had "caused no more stir than a lively dog fight" among the people of the community, and he especially castigated Thomas for not making a stronger effort to remove the prisoners from Lafayette County, even after it became general knowledge that a lynching was in the offing. The correspondent claimed that many people in Lexington knew within two days after Johnson was killed that the wee hours of August 12 was the time appointed for the lynching to occur and that they had been told not to go to bed that night if they wanted to be in on the "fun." If Sheriff Thomas was unaware of the impending tragedy, concluded the correspondent, "he was practically alone in his lack of knowledge."

Chapter Twenty-One

The Most Terrible Deed Ever Committed in Warren County
The Murder of Henry and Nettie Yeater

On Monday, August 31, 1903, rural mail carrier Otto Guggenmoos was running his route in Camp Branch Township northwest of Warrenton, Missouri, when he came to the mailbox of Henry and Nettie Yeater, an elderly couple who had lived in the vicinity for many years. Inside the mailbox Guggenmoos found a mysterious note that read, "Mr. and Mrs. H. W. Yeater have bin killed. Please report." Not quite sure what to make of the note, Guggenmoos showed it to two or three people who lived in the Yeater neighborhood, but they told him it was probably some kind of joke.

The mail carrier wasn't so sure, though, and as it turned out, he was right. The note was anything but a joke.

When he got back to Warrenton late that afternoon, Guggenmoos showed the note to US Marshal William Morsey, who took it more seriously than Yeater's neighbors had. Morsey, who was personally acquainted with Henry Yeater, was concerned enough by the ominous message that he immediately sent a deputy out to Camp Branch with instructions to round up some of Yeater's neighbors and go as a group to check on the old couple.

The small posse went to the Yeater home and, unable to rouse anyone, went inside. Upon entering the bedroom, they discovered what the *Warrenton Herald* described as "a ghastly sight." Sixty-six-year-old Henry Yeater was half-sitting and half-lying in bed, his head and torso bent forward, with his throat cut. At the foot of his bed, his wife, fifty-nine-year-old Henriette "Nettie" Yeater, lay on the floor near the cot where she usually slept. Her throat had been slashed in three or four places, several small cuts were visible on her face and one arm, and her clothes were torn, suggesting that she had struggled with her assailant. Mr. Yeater, who was crippled by inflammatory arthritis, had apparently offered no resistance. The bedroom, according to the *Warrenton Herald*, was "a veritable pool of blood." Both victims were clad in their nightclothes, meaning they had probably been killed during the late night or early morning.

Suspicion immediately settled on twenty-two-year-old William E. Church, the couple's foster son. The note found in the mailbox seemed to match his handwriting, and he had not been seen since the previous afternoon, when neighbor Daniel Buescher saw him in a nearby field dressed in his Sunday clothes.

Mr. and Mrs. Yeater had no children of their own, but they had taken young Church out of the Moberly House of Refuge when he was about nine years old and raised him as their own. He had always been a wild boy and had been sent to reform school at Boonville when he was about fourteen for stealing a gold watch from Mrs. Church's sister, Callie Young. Nettie Church, though, doted on the boy and believed he was innocent. She petitioned the governor to get him released, and he returned home after less than a year at the reformatory.

Now Church had apparently repaid his foster mother's kindness by killing her.

Further investigation seemed to confirm his guilt. A pair of bloody trousers and shoes that were identified as Church's were found beneath a stack of hay in a nearby field, and most of his belongings, including his other clothes, were missing from the house. The house had been ransacked, and various items belonging to Mr. and Mrs. Yeater were also missing.

A young man answering Church's description was seen early Monday morning on Lost Creek several miles south of the Yeater place, and a bloodstained receipt with Mrs. Yeater's name on it was found nearby. The same man, thought to be Church, boarded an eastbound train at Case, in the southwest part of Warren County, but all trace of the suspect was lost after that. Sheriff J. George Polston offered a reward of $500 leading to Church's arrest and conviction.

$500 REWARD!

For the Arrest and Conviction of

William E. Church, CHARGED WITH Murder

of Mr. and Mrs. H. W. Yeater, seven miles north of Warrenton, Mo., on Sunday night, August 30th, 1903.

DESCRIPTION: 5 ft. 6 or 7 inches tall; weight about 160 pounds; about 21 years old; black hair and black eyes; downcast look; poor countenance; criminal look; stoop shouldered; country boy; wore dark clay worsted clothes; black slouch hat. Arrest and notify

J. George Polster,

Sheriff of Warren County.

WARRENTON, MO.

Facsimile of reward notice for Church's arrest. *Warrenton Herald.*

Although a small amount of cash belonging to the Yeaters was missing, no reasonable motive for the murders could be offered, since Yeater had recently made out a will bequeathing all his property to Church upon his and his wife's deaths. In reporting the crime, the *Warrenton Herald* called it "unquestionably the most terrible deed ever committed within the borders of Warren County."

An inquest was held over the Yeaters' bodies early Tuesday morning, September 1. A large crowd gathered the next day for their funeral at Central Grove Church, located near their home in northern Warren County, and they were buried in the adjacent Central Grove Cemetery.

Meanwhile, the train Church had caught at Case arrived in St. Louis at mid-afternoon on Monday, August 31. He promptly bought a ticket for Chicago and left for the Windy City later that evening, arriving on the morning of September 1. For the next few months, Church traveled around the upper Midwest and the Great Lakes area, working on the railroad and at other odd jobs along the way.

During his ramblings, Church wrote a number of defiant letters to various people back in Warren County. From St. Louis, about a month after his flight, he wrote to Sheriff Poston threatening to come back to Warrenton and kill everybody in the town. At Buffalo, New York, the fugitive wrote to John E. "Jack" Young, Mrs. Yeater's brother-in-law, threatening to come back to Warrenton and kill Young. Warren County prosecuting attorney J. B. Garber also received a similar letter from Church, dated St. Paul, Minnesota.

In mid-November, relatives of the Yeaters filed a suit in Warren County Circuit Court asking that Henry Yeater's will be set aside if William E. Church, the current beneficiary, did not appear in the county to claim his inheritance before the next term of court.

On December 22, Church enlisted in the US Marine Corps at Cleveland under the name William Buescher, the same surname as his near neighbor back in Warren County. The new recruit was shipped to League Island Navy Yard in Philadelphia nine days later.

On February 11, 1904, someone wrote from League Island to fifteen-year-old Minnie Roewe of Warren County, giving his name as Lewis A. Laws. He said he'd like to enter into a correspondence with a young woman and that Minnie's name had been recommended to him by fellow marine William Buescher, who supposedly knew Minnie well. Laws inquired as to whether Minnie knew a man who had once worked for her uncle Fritz Buescher. After receiving one or more similar letters from "Laws," Minnie showed them in mid-March to her cousin Daniel Buescher (Fritz's son). Buescher immediately suspected the letters came from Church, and he took them to former prosecuting attorney J. W. Delventhal, who contacted the Philadelphia police. The ex-prosecutor and other investigators thought "Laws" might be an alias Church was using. They conjectured that the former hired hand of Fritz Buescher that the letter writer asked Minnie about was probably Church himself and that the inquiry was an attempt to learn about the status of the murder investigation.

Jack Young assisted Delventhal in following up on the lead furnished by Minnie's letters, and they soon learned from Philadelphia authorities that a man had enlisted in the marines a few months earlier under the name William Buescher and was currently stationed at League Island. Young was convinced that "Buescher" was none other than William Church. Armed with a copy of the warrant for the fugitive's arrest, Young left Warrenton for Philadelphia on March 23 to make a positive identification and have the man taken into custody.

On March 25, Young accompanied Philadelphia police detectives John Lynch and Ed Gallagher to League Island. Young identified the marine calling himself William Buescher as William E. Church, and the detectives had him placed under arrest. Church was temporarily held in the guardhouse at the marine barracks pending authorization for him to be turned over to civil authorities. Notified of the arrest, Sheriff Polster and Prosecuting Attorney Garber secured requisition papers from Missouri governor A. M. Dockery the next day and set out for Philadelphia, arriving on the evening of Sunday the 27th.

On Tuesday, March 29, word came from Washington, D. C. ordering Church's dishonorable discharge and authorizing his transfer to civil authorities. Detectives Lynch and Gallagher immediately went to League Island, and

Church was stripped of his uniform and turned over to the officers. They brought him back to city hall, where he made a full confession of his heinous crime. Describing how he slit the throats of his aged foster parents, Church told the chilling story, according to a Philadelphia correspondent to the *St. Louis Globe-Democrat*, "with the utmost coolness and without expressing the slightest sign of shame."

Church said he got home late on the night of August 30, 1903, and drank a lot of blackberry wine that was in the house. After a brief conversation with Mr. Yeater, Church went into his own room, got his razor from a cigar box where he always kept it, and went back into the Yeaters' bedroom. He cut Mr. Yeater's throat first, and the old man died easily. When he cut Mrs. Yeater's throat, though, she rose up in bed, yelled, and tried to put up a fight. Church slashed her two or three more times, and she fell off her cot screaming. He cut her several more times as she lay weltering on the floor, and she finally succumbed.

The murderer then went into his room, put some of his things into a grip or valise, wrote a note for the mailman, and took off. He changed clothes in a nearby cornfield and then walked and trotted through the darkness as he made his way toward Gore, where he caught a train for St. Louis. (Initial reports in the wake of the murders said the suspect caught a train at nearby Case. It's unclear whether the initial reports were wrong or Church was wrong in his confession.)

Church said he'd been thinking about killing the couple for four years, because he was convinced they weren't going to leave him any money. Unbeknown to him, though, they had already done so at the time of his crime.

The day after his confession, March 30, Church was heavily shackled, placed on a train, and escorted back to Missouri by Sheriff Polster and Prosecutor Garber, with Jack Young riding in a separate car of the same train. During the trip, Church again talked freely of his vicious crime. He said he had argued with his foster parents on the night of the crime and then and there made up his mind to kill them. He took only twenty dollars from the Yeater premises, because that was all the money he could find. Church also explained that Lewis Laws was, in fact, a fellow marine and not just an alias he had adopted. Laws was getting ready to ship out to the Philippines, and Church had given him Minnie Roewe's name so that he could write to her after he was overseas. Laws, though, had gone ahead and written to her while he was still at League Island, and Church was afraid to tell him not to, for fear that Laws would get suspicious.

The train arrived in St. Louis that night, and Polster turned the prisoner over to city officers to be held in the Four Courts Jail for safekeeping until his appearance in Warren County Circuit Court. Church was placed in a cell adjoining that of the notorious Bill "The Missouri Kid" Rudolph, the same cell previously occupied by Rudolph's partner in crime, George Collins, who had been recently hanged.

While he was in custody at St. Louis, Church again talked about the murders. He claimed that a relative of the Yeaters had promised him $500 to get the old couple out of the way so that the kinsman could inherit their money. This was an attempt to implicate Jack Young in the crime, because Church resented Young for having put him in the reformatory for stealing Mrs. Young's watch, but the story was summarily dismissed. Shortly after Church's arrival in St. Louis, at least two city newspapers did write-ups about the murders, accompanied by a photograph of the criminal, and Church "seemed tickled to see his picture in the papers."

Church retained Claude R. Ball as his lawyer by signing over the property Henry Yeater had willed to him, and the Yeater relatives agreed to drop their suit seeking the property.

On the morning of April 18, Church was brought to Warrenton for arraignment. A large crowd had gathered near the courthouse to get a glimpse of the notorious murderer, and when Church was escorted through the crowd, he smiled and, recognizing an old acquaintance, hailed him with a warm "Hello" as though unconcerned about his present circumstance.

Attorney Ball entered a plea of not guilty on behalf of his client. Prosecutor Garber said he'd be ready for trial in two weeks, but Ball said he needed until July to prepare. The judge compromised, setting June 20 as the date for trial to begin. Later that day, Church was taken back to St. Louis to await the trial.

It began on Monday, June 20, as scheduled, and a large crowd again flocked to Warrenton for the occasion. Defense attorney Ball filed a motion to disqualify Judge Johnson, the regular circuit judge for Warren County, but Johnson and Prosecutor Garber, anticipating such a move, had already summoned Judge Nat Shelton of Macon as a replacement. The defense objected to Shelton as well, but he was appointed to hear the case anyway when the two sides could not agree on another judge.

On Tuesday, Ball filed a motion alleging that Church was insane and incapable of aiding in his own defense. He sought an inquiry into Church's sanity and a continuance to allow more time to prepare his defense. The motion was denied on the grounds that the defense failed to show the alleged insanity had developed since the crime was committed. If Church was insane at the time of the crime, Ball could argue insanity as a defense, but that was no reason to delay the trial.

Ball next asked for a continuance on the grounds that he had no idea that Judge Shelton would be on hand to replace Judge Johnson and that he, therefore, did not expect to have to be ready for trial. Shelton overruled the motion, saying that Johnson had every right to call any judge he saw fit and that the defense should have been ready.

Intent on securing a continuance, Ball objected to the wording of the indictment, but this objection was also overruled. Finally, he said he needed a continuance of at least five to ten days to round up certain witnesses for the defense, particularly Church's mother, and the judge granted an extension until the following Monday with the stipulation that jury selection would go forward in the meantime.

When court resumed on Monday morning, June 27, attendance was large but not as large as it had been early the previous week because farmers were busy harvesting wheat and tending other crops. The defense made yet another attempt to delay the proceedings, filing a motion for a special inquiry into Church's sanity, but Shelton denied this motion, too, saying the issue had already been settled. Ball continued his stalling tactics, requesting a continuance on the grounds that an important defense witness was in Vernon County with a broken arm and unable to travel. Shelton thought this was a lame excuse and ordered that the Vernon County sheriff be contacted and the witness summoned to Warren County at once.

The trial finally got underway later on Monday with opening statements. When Prosecutor Garber mentioned the letters Church had written threatening to return to Warren County and kill local citizens, the defendant smiled broadly as though the whole thing was a joke. However, he did show the first signs of nervousness as Garber detailed the murder of the Yeaters. In his opening statement, Ball indirectly admitted that his client had committed the murders, but he expected to show that Church was not guilty by reason of insanity.

The prosecution witnesses were mainly people who had been involved in discovering and investigating the crime or in apprehending the suspect. Garber also called several expert witnesses to blunt the insanity argument he anticipated from the defense. One such witness was R. E. Graham, who, as the Yeaters' family physician, had also treated Church. The doctor said he considered Church a moral degenerate who was destitute of principle. Ball tried to get Graham to admit that moral degeneracy and mental degeneracy were the same, but the doctor rejected such an equivalency.

The prosecution's case resumed on Tuesday morning, and then the defense commenced its case later the same day.

Among the witnesses was Lyman Drake, superintendent of the boys' reformatory at Boonville. Drake testified that while Church was at the reformatory, he was addicted to self-abuse (i.e. masturbation), and it became necessary to put night gloves on him. Drake considered the boy mentally unbalanced, but on cross-examination, he admitted that Church would not have been allowed to remain at the reformatory if he'd been deemed insane. Two St. Louis jailers also testified as to having witnessed Church's masturbation. They said that he seemed to have no shame about it and that he also displayed other peculiar behavior.

A number of people who'd known Church as a child or youth, including one of his teachers, testified that he was not popular because he was hard to get along with and often bullied other kids. Witnesses told of having seen Church kill a dog, break windows out of buildings, and deliberately turn over a baby buggy with the infant in the carriage. Upon cross examination, though, nearly all the witnesses admitted that they attributed Church's misbehavior to meanness rather than insanity.

On Wednesday, the defense trotted several expert witnesses to the stand to testify to Church's insanity. The essence of their testimony was that Church was so addicted to certain "bad habits" that his mind had become affected and he'd become mentally deficient to the point that he was not responsible for anything he might do. In rebuttal, the state offered several expert witnesses of its own who testified that the fact that Church "had been guilty of excessive masturbation did not indicate that defendant's mind was impaired nor that he had any mental trouble whatever." Most of the day on Wednesday was taken up by this duel of experts over the effect Church's masturbation might have on his mind. Having been forewarned of the "unavoidable vulgarity," the "gentler sex...retired and absented themselves from the courtroom" throughout the day.

William Church, circa 1907. *St. Louis Post-Dispatch.*

The trial concluded with closing arguments on Thursday, June 30. The jury came back later the same day, after a brief deliberation, with a verdict finding Church guilty of murder in the first degree. The defense petitioned for a new trial, and imposition of sentence was suspended until after the motion could be heard. On August 23, Judge Shelton denied the motion for a new trial and pronounced sentence: death by hanging on October 14, 1904. The defense immediately appealed the verdict to the Missouri Supreme Court, automatically staying the execution.

The high court finally took up the Church case at its October 1906 term. The defense's bill of exceptions contained fourteen points, including arguments that Church should have been granted a separate sanity hearing before the trial began, that Judge Shelton should not have been seated as a replacement judge, that the prosecutor's reference to the defendant as a "culprit" had prejudiced the jury, and that Church should have been granted a new trial based on new evidence. Calling the murder of the Yeaters "unsurpassed in atrociousness by any crime ever committed in this commonwealth," the justices rejected the defense's arguments and affirmed the lower court's decision. The ruling was handed down on December 22, and a new execution date was set for January 10, 1907, in Warrenton. A last-minute appeal by Church's attorney to Missouri governor Joseph W. Folk to open an inquiry into the condemned man's sanity was rejected.

On the evening before his date with death, Church talked freely of his crime. He said he regretted the deed and wasn't sure why he did it, except that he'd argued with his foster parents continually in the weeks leading up to the crime and had argued with them again on the fateful night. He admitted that his previous claim that Jack Young had paid him to commit the crime was not true. Church's last request was that his brother, who was then in the reformatory at Boonville, be taught to lead a better life than he did.

On the morning of the 10th, Church walked to the scaffold "with a steady step and did not show the least sign of weakening," according to the *St. Louis Post-Dispatch*. He dropped through the trap at 9:11 a.m. and was pronounced dead eighteen and a half minutes later. According to his request, his body was turned over to the Catholic Church and buried in the local Catholic cemetery.

Chapter Twenty-Two

The Mystery of Pine Flat
Texas County's Hotbed Murder

After thirty-six-year-old Gilbert Hall was arrested for murder in Texas County, Missouri, in February 1920, he maintained a total silence regarding the crime. He'd lived in the county only a few months, having moved in with his victim, fifty-eight-year-old Frank Elliott, on a forty-acre farm south of Cabool the previous fall, but little else was known about him. Once in custody, Hall started growing a beard, and any time he was taken out of jail, he became "uneasy and restless," according to the *Houston Herald*. He would pull his coat collar up and his hat brim down, and if anyone tried to snap a picture of him, he would put his hands up in front of his face. A number of Hall's letters were found in the shack he and Elliott had shared five miles south of town, but all of them were signed only with a capital "M" or "C." All through the letters there was "a secrecy about names," with only initials being used for both people and places. There was "a mystery about Hall," concluded the *Herald*, which he seemed to be trying to cover up in the letters.

As it turned out, there was good reason why the prisoner didn't want to have his picture taken or to talk about his past, because Frank Elliott was not the first person he'd killed. Hall had escaped less than a year earlier from the Kansas State Prison at Lansing, and if he was recognized, he'd be sent back for sure to serve the rest of his life sentence, even if he somehow wriggled out of his present predicament.

Standing six feet, seven inches tall, Hall found it hard to conceal his identity for long, however, and authorities soon learned his real name was Samuel Bitler. Also known by the alias Carl Morton, Bitler had raped and killed a woman in Kansas over ten years earlier.

On Saturday, May 16, 1908, Mrs. Susan Rosenberger, who lived about seven miles northwest of Belvidere, Kansas, drove to town in a spring wagon to do some shopping. She started for home about five o'clock in the afternoon but didn't show up in a timely fashion. During the intense search that followed, her body was found the next day half a mile off the main road in a deep gulch about four miles west of Belvidere. She had been sexually assaulted and then shot three times. It was theorized that the assailant had raped the woman and then killed her to keep her from identifying him.

Some men who'd been fishing in the area of the crime came forward as witnesses. They had heard three shots coming from the direction where the body was later found, and just after the gunshots, they saw a man wearing dark clothes ride swiftly away on an iron gray horse. Investigators followed the gray horse, which left a peculiar hoof print, to a nearby farm where Sam Bitler was working. Based on the hoof mark and other circumstantial evidence, Bitler was arrested and charged with murder.

Bitler's trial in February 1909 ended in a mistrial when the jury split eight for conviction and four for acquittal, but upon retrial in March he was convicted of first degree murder. His lawyers planned to appeal the verdict, but Bitler escaped in June before the petition could be filed. He was recaptured in Memphis, Tennessee, about the first of August and brought back to Kansas. His escape had nullified his right to an appeal; so he was promptly forwarded to the state prison in Lansing.

On the afternoon of May 28, 1919, after having served about ten years in prison, Bitler and two other inmates escaped from the Lansing facility by slipping away from a guard while on a work detail. Just a few months later, Bitler showed up in Texas County under the name Gilbert Hall and initiated talks with Frank Elliott about purchasing Elliott's farm in the Pine Flat neighborhood five miles south of Cabool near the Douglas County line.

After returning to Kansas City, where he'd been hiding out, Hall tried to get Elliott to come to Kansas City, also, to complete the land transaction, but Elliott refused. Having somehow got hold of a wad of money, Hall traveled back to Cabool in October and paid Elliott $1,800 in one-hundred dollar bills. Although Hall now owned the property, Elliott stayed on at the farm through some sort of arrangement between the two men.

On January 26, 1920, neighbor Everett Thompson called at the Hall farm to accompany Frank Elliott to nearby Pine Flat Baptist Church, as he was wont to do, but Hall told Thompson that Elliott was not home and had "gone south." During their conversation, Hall mentioned that he had shot at a dog the night before and thought he'd hit the animal because there was blood on the porch. Thompson came back a few days later and noticed that one side of the front porch had been recently scrubbed clean. Asked about Elliott, Hall repeated his story that he had gone south.

Another neighbor, Albert Reed, also paid a visit to the Hall place in late January and was told that Elliott had gone south. Reed noticed that Hall had been digging in the ground, and he asked him what he was doing. Hall replied that he was making a hotbed. Reed remarked that it was a little early for a hotbed, and Hall replied, "I want to be early." When Reed returned a few days later and inquired about Elliott, Hall clarified Elliott's whereabouts, saying he had "gone to Arkansas."

During late January and early February 1920, Hall forged Elliott's name on a number of checks and cashed them on Elliott's account at the First National Bank in Cabool. He used the money to purchase a horse and buggy, home furnishings, and a number of other items. On the morning of February 10, Hall showed back up at the First National Bank and presented a couple of more checks that had been written on Elliott's account and made out to Hall. Cashier Robert W. Clifton went ahead and cashed the checks, but he'd begun to get suspicious because Elliott's signature didn't seem quite right and the cashier had learned that Elliott had supposedly left Cabool.

After cashing the checks, Clifton reported his suspicions to Texas County sheriff Jack McCaskill. The sheriff and Deputy Dick Stogsdill located Hall at Patton's Hardware Store. When he denied any knowledge of Elliott's whereabouts, they placed him under arrest on suspicion. Although armed with a revolver and two long knives, the suspect offered no resistance.

With Hall detained temporarily at Cabool, a search party consisting of Sheriff McCaskill, Deputy Stogsdill, Prosecuting Attorney George Scott, and G. W. Duncan went out to the Hall farm to look for any sign of Elliott. They noticed the hotbed behind the house and could tell that it had been made recently. Procuring spades and shovels, they started digging and came upon Elliott's body just a couple of feet beneath the surface. The head appeared to have been crushed by a blunt instrument, and the face was bruised beyond recognition. The body was wrapped in a blanket that apparently had come from the bed where both Hall and Elliott slept, and there were straps positioned around the body as though they had been used to carry it and lower it into the shallow grave.

The search party at once returned to Cabool to question Hall. He refused to talk about the crime except to deny knowledge of it, and he was retained in the city jail at Cabool. Elliott's body was brought to Cabool, and a coroner's inquest was held the next day, February 11. The jurors found that the disfigurement, which had initially been attributed to a blunt instrument, was instead caused by moles or rodents eating at the face and that death was caused by three gunshots to the head. The bullets were .32 caliber, and the revolver Hall had in his possession when he was arrested was a .32 caliber. The jury concluded that Elliott had come to his death by gunfire at the hands of Gilbert Hall, and Hall was moved to the Texas County Jail at Houston to await a preliminary hearing.

Further investigation at the Hall farm turned up the cryptic correspondence between "M" and "C." M appeared to be a young woman, while C referred to Hall. In one of the letters, M cautioned C to "be careful," and the couple appeared to be making plans to get married. Shortly after his arrest, Hall requested that May Dale of Peoria, Illinois, be notified; so it was deduced that May was the mysterious Miss M. Authorities in Peoria were contacted, and she was questioned but apparently was never arrested, as Hall did not implicate her in the crime in any way.

The search of the premises at the Hall farm also revealed blood stains on the mattress of the bed where the two men slept, and a pair of bloody overalls that were identified as Elliott's were found in the house. Heavy tracks led back and forth between the house and the hotbed. Investigators concluded that Elliott had been shot while lying in the bed and carried to the makeshift grave. Hall had apparently continued to sleep in the bloody deathbed even after the murder.

On February 21, Hall was brought back to Cabool for a preliminary hearing before Justice of the Peace A. N. Dove. The room where the examination was held, according to a Springfield newspaper, "was inadequate to accommodate the large crowd of farmers who were in Cabool to hear the trial." Sheriff McCaskill recounted the circumstances of Hall's arrest and the evidence uncovered at the Hall farm after the arrest. Everett Thompson, Albert Reed, and one other man recalled Elliott's disappearance on or about January 26 and told of Hall's suspicious behavior after the disappearance. At the end of the hearing, Hall was bound over to await trial at the April term of the Texas County Circuit Court, and he was taken back to the jail at Houston.

Although Hall remained close-mouthed about his background, efforts to determine his origins continued. In mid-April, J. A. Roman, the chief of police of Eureka, Kansas, came to Houston and identified Hall as Samuel L. Bitler, who was originally from Eureka and whose mother still lived there. Bitler, the officer said, had been sent to the Kansas State Penitentiary for murder over ten years ago and had escaped less than a year ago. However, Missouri authorities chose to proceed with their case against Hall rather than turn him over to Kansas.

Hall's trial got underway at Houston on April 19, and lasted four days. The court room was crowded at all times, and the feeling against Hall/Bitler was intense throughout the proceeding, especially when Chief of Police Roman took the stand to identify Hall as an escapee from the Kansas State Penitentiary. On Thursday, April 22, the jury came back with a verdict finding the defendant guilty of second-degree murder and sentencing him to life imprisonment. A report leaked out that, when deliberations began, as many as five jurors were ready to convict Hall of first-degree murder and sentence him to hang, while one or two held out for acquittal. The second-degree murder verdict was thus reached as a sort of compromise. "It is always a hard matter," opined the *Houston Herald*, "to secure a verdict for capital punishment on circumstantial evidence." According to the *Herald*, the prosecution was also limited as to how much they could reveal about Hall's criminal past, since he had declined to take the stand as a witness in his own defense.

Hall was taken back to his cell at the Texas County Jail. The following Monday, April 26, 1920, he was transferred to the Missouri State Penitentiary at Jefferson City. He died in the prison hospital on December 4, 1929, from tuberculosis.

Chapter Twenty-Three

For God's Sake, Give Me a Chance
The Lynching of Walter Mitchell

On Thursday evening August 6, 1925, twenty-one-year-old Leonard Utt and his teenage girlfriend, Maud Holt, attended a social event at Excelsior Springs, Missouri. About midnight, as Leonard was driving the girl to her home near Lawson, several miles north of Excelsior Springs, a man waved the couple down with a flashlight. When Leonard slowed to a halt, a black man about thirty years old jumped on the running board of the vehicle and struck the driver a hard blow with the flashlight, knocking him senseless.

The assailant then dragged the girl from the automobile and forced her into the backseat. As the man began to assault Maud, her screams and flailing frightened the attacker off, and he fled toward Excelsior Springs. Recovering from the blow he'd received, Leonard delivered the young woman to her nearby home, and the couple reported the attack to the girl's father, Charles N. Holt.

Outraged by the news, Holt immediately organized a posse, which included his sons and Utt, to track down the villain. Following the assailant's tracks, which were distinctive in that his shoes had no heels, the search party found a black man asleep in a small, vacant house in Excelsior Springs about daylight on August 7. Leonard Utt identified the man as the person who had struck him and assaulted Maud. Near the sleeping man lay a flashlight that was presumed to be the one with which the attacker had hit Utt.

The suspect was taken to the city jail in Excelsior Springs, where he was identified as Walter Mitchell (aka Miller Mitchell), a thirty-three-year-old black man who was originally from Meridian, Mississippi. He had come north about ten years earlier and had a wife living in St. Paul, Minnesota.

Maud Holt was summoned to Excelsior Springs, and she, too, identified Mitchell as the man who had attacked her. Maud retired to the matron's quarters at the jail, and Mitchell's arraignment on an assault charge was set for 2:00 p.m. that afternoon.

As word of the attack on Maud and the identification of a suspect spread, angry citizens, many of them from the Lawson area, poured into Excelsior Springs throughout the morning of August 7. Milling around outside the jail, the mob remained mostly sullen rather than boisterous, but an occasional cry of "Bring him out!" came from the crowd.

As the mob increased in numbers and became more threatening, Chief of Police John F. Craven and eight or ten deputies, who were watching the prisoner, attempted to remove him to safety by way of a basement door, but they turned back when they found the door heavily guarded by members of the mob.

Shortly before noon, Clay County prosecutor Raymond Cummins, who had been in court at Liberty during the morning, was notified of the tense situation in Excelsior Springs, and he set out immediately for the scene. Upon his arrival, the mob surrounded his automobile and tore the wiring from the car as he made his way to the city hall. Stepping back out among the throng, Cummins pled with the members of the mob not to resort to violence. He said the prisoner would not be turned over to them and that he was there to see that the law took its course.

Shortly afterward, Cummins organized a committee of citizens and law officers to speak directly with Charles Holt, Maud's father. Holt was brought into the city hall, where Cummins proposed to take Mitchell to safety, and he asked Holt to join the escort.

"Stay with them, Holt!" cried a voice from the mob outside the building.

Whether the shout of encouragement bolstered the father's resolve not to give in to the committee's appeals is uncertain, but Holt declined the invitation to help escort Mitchell to safety.

After Holt was dismissed, it became increasingly apparent that the vigilantes would attempt to take the law into their own hands, and a small party of officers and other defenders gathered in a large room at the jail adjoining Mitchell's cell. They wedged a two-by-four against the outside door to reinforce its flimsy lock.

About 2:00 p.m., Cummins, realizing that mob action was imminent if something was not done to prevent it, called the Kansas City police and asked them to send reinforcements. A riot squad of over fifty officers was dispatched to Excelsior Springs.

Before they could arrive, however, the mob, now numbering about 500 men, decided to act. The decision was no doubt hastened by the news that police reinforcements were on the way. A fire station was housed in a large room of the city hall building adjoining the jail, and, shortly before 3:00 p.m., someone in the mob turned in a false fire alarm. When a fire truck roared out of the building, the vigilantes, one of whom carried a sledgehammer, rushed into the building through the open door, gaining access to an interior door that led directly to the jail.

The mob streamed through the interior door into the large room that fronted the cells. The man with the sledge went to work on the lock of Mitchell's cell as the prisoner, already handcuffed, quaked in fear. The heavy hammer made short work of the lock, and the mob surged in and dragged Mitchell outside, brushing aside a token resistance from the guards.

Despite being handcuffed, Mitchell screamed and resisted as he was dragged into the street, and when some of the mob began beating him, he tried vainly to fight back. A few bloodthirsty vigilantes yelled, "Burn him!" but most of the lawless horde seemed to have settled on hanging. A few men lifted the prisoner above their heads and started off down the street with him, carrying him a short distance in that manner before setting him back down and forcing him to walk.

"Down Thompson avenue, south on Elms boulevard past the fashionable Elms hotel, and farther south down Kansas City avenue to the edge of town the howling procession led him," said a contemporaneous newspaper report.

Excelsior Springs was a noted mineral-water resort town, and the Elms Hotel was perhaps its most popular destination. From the verandas of the hotel, "wealthy tourists and health seekers" gawked at the terrible parade as it passed.

Someone in the mob procured a rope during the march, and it was fastened around the doomed man's neck as he was dragged along. "In the crowd," according to an Associated Press report, "were many women, some of them leading children, who to keep pace with the rapid strides of their mothers, had to trot beside them." Another account said only that a "sprinkling" of women followed on the fringes of the mob.

The vigilantes halted at an oak tree on the south edge of town, near where Kansas City Avenue ended at the Wabash Railroad, and many in the unholy throng swelled across the track, forcing a passenger train to stop. One of the leaders of the mob asked Mitchell if he had anything to say, and he replied, "Yes, I'm guilty, but for God's sake give me a chance."

But the ruthless mob had no intention of giving Mitchell a chance. The captive spectators aboard the train watched in horror as one of the gang climbed up the oak tree and tossed the other end of the rope over a high limb. While the man was climbing the tree, Samuel J. Rowell, an Excelsior Springs attorney, pleaded with the would-be lynchers not to take the law into their own hands, but his voice was scarcely audible above the howling of the mob. Finally, one of the vigilantes turned to the lawyer and shouted, "You'll be next if you don't get away from here."

Mitchell continued to squirm and moan, even as "willing hands" drew him up, several feet into the air. He died, though, within three or four minutes, and the mob promptly dispersed.

The first police reinforcements from Kansas City arrived about ten minutes too late to prevent the lynching. They cut down Mitchell's body, and it was taken to a local undertaker's office, where a long line of people stood in the street outside waiting to view it. Perhaps only a "sprinkling" of women had followed on the outskirts of the mob to witness the lynching, but many more now took the opportunity to gape at the victim after he was dead. Mitchell was later buried in Elmwood Cemetery in Excelsior Springs.

Clay County officials declined to investigate the lynching. Coroner H. W. Hill signed Mitchell's death certificate without conducting an inquest, giving the cause of death as "hanged by a mob, parties unknown." Prosecutor Cummins said, "We feel that justice has been done. Of course, the method was crude. I would have preferred that the Negro could have been hanged legally and I am convinced that it would have been done."

Interviewed the day after the lynching, Cummins added that he didn't know who the members of the mob were and that he had been unable to find out. To a different reporter, Cummins said he was trying to investigate the incident but that he was "up against a rock wall." He said nobody knew who was in the mob or at least nobody was telling.

Police Chief Craven, on the other hand, said he knew the identity of some of the members of the mob but that it was up to the prosecutor to bring charges. Other city officials and the businessmen of Excelsior Springs, concerned about the lynching's negative reflection on their town's reputation as a resort destination, were also quick to blame Cummins and the county for not responding in a more forceful manner to prevent the mob action.

Cummins retorted that Craven and other Excelsior Springs officials were just trying to pass the buck. As criticism against the prosecutor mounted, however, including a reprimand from the Missouri attorney general, Cummins promised to call a grand jury to inquire into the lynching, and he also authorized Craven to conduct an independent investigation into the matter. The Excelsior Springs Chamber of Commerce announced it was considering conducting its own investigation.

The Kansas City branch of the NAACP filed a formal protest with Missouri governor Samuel Baker in connection with the lynching. A telegram was also sent to the National Crime Commission urging an investigation into the extralegal execution.

On Monday, August 10, Governor Baker ordered his attorney general to investigate Mitchell's lynching and to assist Cummins in prosecuting those responsible for the vigilante outbreak. The promised grand jury got underway later in the week, but it was discharged the following week after more than 100 witnesses were examined and "no one remembered who actually pulled the rope that took Mitchell's life."

Chapter Twenty-Four

Comin' to No Good End
The Kidnapping and Murder of Dr. J. C. B. Davis

About 5:00 o'clock Tuesday afternoon, January 26, 1937, as Dr. J. C. B. Davis of Willow Springs, Missouri, was leaving his office, he was approached by a young man who, according to a bystander nearby, said that his name was "Mr. James" and that his wife was sick at his home south of town and needed the doctor's help. Davis stepped back into his office and asked his secretary, Geraldine Frommell, to call his wife and let her know he'd be an hour or so late getting home. After Dr. Davis rejoined the stranger at the doorway, they stepped into the street, where the doctor retrieved a medical bag containing emergency supplies from his vehicle. The two men then got into the stranger's vehicle and left.

It was the last time anyone saw Dr. Davis alive.

Although it was not a normal practice for the doctor to leave in another person's car rather than take his own vehicle when he made house calls, no one thought much about the incident until early the next morning when Dr. Davis had still not come home and his car was found still parked near his office in Willow Springs with his surgical kit inside. His wife promptly notified authorities that he was missing, and the Missouri State Highway Patrol began an investigation.

The stranger's automobile was described as a 1936 or 1937 Ford. The young man himself was said to weigh about 135 pounds and to be about twenty-five years old, about five feet nine inches in height, dark complexioned, and wearing a zippered leather jacket, blue trousers, and a gray felt hat. One or two people living south of Willow Springs reported possible sightings of the stranger's vehicle, but no solid leads into the doctor's disappearance were developed on Wednesday.

Dr. Davis had planned to withdraw a large sum of money from a Willow Springs bank on Tuesday afternoon to be paid to relatives as settlement of his nephew's estate, although a cashier had persuaded him to leave the money on deposit for the time being. Initial theories of the apparent crime included the possibility that his abductor knew of the proposed estate settlement and had kidnapped him for the money.

Another early theory was that the abductor was a member of an outlaw gang who'd taken the doctor to a secret hideout to treat a wounded gang member. There was no evidence to support either theory, and law officers were skeptical of both.

When a ransom note was received at the Davis home on Thursday the 28th, FBI agents were summoned to Willow Springs to join the investigation, because the note, postmarked at West Plains, had been sent through the US Mail. Opening with the salutation "Dear friend," the letter was written in the doctor's handwriting, meaning the kidnapper had forced Davis to write his own ransom letter. It demanded that $5,000 be paid in four $1,000 bills, nine $100 bills, and five $20 bills. It threatened the doctor with death if the family did not comply, and it contained instructions for delivering the money. The note was signed, "The Kidnaper." Receipt of the letter and many other details of the case were not made public at first for fear of endangering Dr. Davis's life or otherwise hampering the investigation.

On Friday, January 29, a young man named Buster Brixey discovered Davis's medical kit caught in some brush of the North Fork River about thirteen miles southwest of Willow Springs. Wading out to get it, he took it to a nearby

CCC camp, and officials there summoned the highway patrol to come and get the bag.

The discovery of the medical bag, containing the doctor's prescription pad and other items, raised fears that Davis had already been foully dealt with. Nevertheless his son-in-law, following the ransom letter's instructions, drove along the road between Willow Springs and Ava about midnight Saturday evening looking for a white flag that the letter said would mark the spot where the ransom money was to be dropped, but the son-in-law, his vision obscured by heavy fog, failed to find a white flag.

Investigators were operating on the theory that the kidnapper acted alone and that he was a small-time crook. "It seems unlikely that a professional gangster would do some of the things this man has done," said Missouri State Highway Patrol colonel B. Marvin Casteel. One of the things that seemed out of character for a professional criminal was the demand that the ransom money be paid mostly in $1,000 bills, because currency of such denomination would be hard to pass.

On Monday morning, February 2, Davis's wife received a second note at her home in Willow Springs, written in unfamiliar handwriting, renewing the demand for $5,000 in ransom and directing that it should be delivered along the road at 9:00 p.m. February 4th in the same manner as demanded in the first letter. It, like the first note, was signed, "The Kidnaper."

Meanwhile at about the same time the second note was received, highway patrol officers received a promising tip from a person who had seen the doctor and the young man in an automobile together on the day of the doctor's disappearance. Lawmen located an automobile matching the witness's description at the home of Samuel Kenyon in Grimmet, a small community northwest of West Plains about halfway between West Plains and the North Fork River, where the medical bag was found.

Officers identified Kenyon's twenty-one-year-old son, Robert, as a suspect in the kidnapping. Young Kenyon was in possession of a .25 caliber automatic pistol, and it was determined that the suspect automobile found on the premises had been stolen from Rolla in November of the previous year, about the same time Kenyon turned up in Grimmet with it. In addition, a notebook pad with paper that appeared to match the paper on which the second note was written was found in Kenyon's suitcase.

Kenyon denied knowledge of the kidnaping, but he was arrested and taken back to Willow Springs for questioning. Under intense grilling, Kenyon continued to assert his innocence, until FBI agents were able to determine that indentations on the top sheet of the notepad matched the writing on the second ransom note. Confronted with this evidence by Colonel Casteel nineteen hours into the interrogation, young Kenyon stared at it for a minute in silence before saying, "You've got me." He then confessed to kidnapping and murdering Davis and offered to take the officers to where the body was.

According to local lore, two officers finally got Kenyon to confess by taking him handcuffed out into the ice-cold North Fork River up to his waist or beyond. One officer would hold the prisoner in the water while the other returned to the bank to warm himself beside a big bonfire, and they continued taking turns in this manner until Kenyon cracked. The official story at the time, however, was simply that Kenyon broke down and confessed when faced with the overwhelming evidence of the notepad.

In the pre-dawn darkness of February 3, Kenyon led authorities about twelve miles south of Willow Springs to a brushy area just off Highway 63 near Olden, Missouri, and pointed "indifferently" to the body, which was face down clutching a pair of gloves in one hand and a checkbook in the other. It was concluded upon close inspection and further investigation that the doctor had been killed shortly after he was kidnapped, having been shot while in the act of trying to write a check to pay his own ransom. Kenyon admitted he'd killed Davis with the automatic pistol authorities had earlier taken from him, and the only explanation he could offer for his desperate deed was that he wanted money so that he and his girlfriend could get married.

Kenyon was taken back to Willow Springs and then, still in the early-morning hours, whisked away to the Jackson County Jail in Kansas City to avert possible mob action. Dr. Davis was much respected in the community, and his kidnapping had aroused the citizens to a fever pitch. Law officers knew an announcement that he'd been killed and that a suspect in his murder had been arrested might be the tipping point.

Later in the day on February 3, a coroner's inquest was conducted on Davis's body, and the examination determined that the doctor had been shot twice in the head and four times in the body. Tests later confirmed that the pistol taken from Kenyon was the murder weapon.

Also on the 3rd, Opal Welch, Kenyon's eighteen-year-old girlfriend living near Dora, was picked up for questioning.

Although he'd previously confessed, Kenyon changed his tune once he reached Kansas City. Questioned on the 4th, he now denied all knowledge of the kidnapping and murder. He admitted he'd written the second ransom note, but he said he'd done so only under duress. According to the suspect's new story, a mysterious man he'd met at a café in West Plains was aware that Kenyon had stolen the automobile in Rolla and threatened to turn him in if he didn't agree to write the note and help retrieve the ransom. Kenyon said the man resembled his own physical appearance except that he was about five years older than Kenyon. The man had borrowed Kenyon's hat and coat on occasion, and he had also borrowed Kenyon's automobile several times. Kenyon said he knew the man only as "Nighthawk," a name he'd adopted because of his nocturnal roving. According to the prisoner, putting out the white flag along the road, as described in the ransom notes, was the Nighthawk's idea but that he (Kenyon) had not carried out the plan on the night first designated because of the heavy traffic along the road that evening.

The officers in Kansas City fed Kenyon well and offered him small inducements like chewing tobacco and cigars as they interrogated him. The prisoner refused the chew but took a cigar and puffed on it as he answered their questions. "You-all sure are mighty generous fellers around here," he remarked, "but you all can't help me much unless you catch this Nighthawk feller."

When he wasn't answering the law officers' questions, Kenyon spent his time writing love letters to Opal. "Dear Opal," he wrote, "I still love you. I am in jail at Kansas City but don't you get worried. They picked you up out of meanness. They got your name from a mill sales tax token I carried in my pocket. I am innocent. I don't know when the trial will be held, but it will be in Howell County. Love and kisses, Bob."

While Robert Kenyon was being grilled by law officers in Kansas City, a newspaper reporter called at his home in Grimmet to interview his parents. Neither his father, sixty-two-year-old Samuel, nor his mother, fifty-eight-year-old Sophie, tried to deny their son's involvement in the crime of which he had been accused, although they insisted he must have had an accomplice. "Seems as like he just naturally was a lughead," Samuel said of his son. "Many's the time I'd a told him he was a-comin' to no good end." Likening Robert to gangsters Pretty Boy Floyd and John Dillinger, the old man said "fellers like that" were born with an innate meanness. "It's just in 'em."

"You don't know nowadays," Sophie added with a sob, "what the hell yore raisin' 'em up for—the pen, the rope, or what. I declare I never thought about that boy o' mine a-doin' sech a caper."

Mr. Kenyon said he knew something was wrong when Robert came home with the new vehicle telling a wild story that a secret service company in St. Louis had furnished it to him. Sam said he tried to talk to his son, but it did no good. "I'm 62 now, and I never was arrested or got into any kind of trouble," he said. "And we never raised our children up for any card table or dance hall."

Unlike Kenyon's parents, both FBI agents and local law officers were convinced the suspect had acted alone. Unimpressed by his fantastic tale about the Nighthawk, they pronounced the investigation closed.

Released after questioning, Opal Welch was interviewed at her parents' farm near Dora on Friday morning, February 5. She told reporters that she and young Kenyon had planned to be married the previous Saturday. Asserting her boyfriend's innocence, she said Robert was "too tenderhearted to do a thing like that."

The same morning, Buster Brixey, the young man who'd found Dr. Davis's medical bag, was picked up for questioning, because authorities had learned that he was a friend of Kenyon's. He was released shortly afterward when it was determined that, although the two had once been pretty good friends, they had not associated with each other in two or three years.

The doctor's funeral service was also held on February 5, in the afternoon. All stores in Willow Springs closed during the service, which was held in the high school auditorium to accommodate the large crowd, estimated at 1,800 people. After the service, Dr. Davis was interred in the Willow Springs City Cemetery.

On February 11, Kenyon retracted his story about the Nighthawk and confessed that he alone had killed Dr. Davis. He said he'd stopped and forced the doctor to write the first ransom note a few miles south of Willow Springs and then had taken him to the isolated spot near Olden and killed him about 45 minutes after the abduction, as the pleading Davis tried to write a $5,000 check in barter for his life. The only reason he could give for the killing was that he didn't know where to keep his captive.

Robert Kenyon in his Kansas City jail cell. *St. Louis Star and Times*.

On February 18, Kenyon was taken from Kansas City to West Plains for his preliminary hearing. He waived examination and was promptly taken back to Kansas City to await trial in June on a charge of first-degree murder. In late May he was brought back to West Plains and lodged in the new Howell County Jail. A change of venue to Oregon County was granted in early June, and the trial, originally scheduled for the 15th, was reset for July.

In early July, Opal Welch was allowed to visit her beau through a small opening in his cell at the West Plains jail. It was the first time she'd seen him since his arrest.

Kenyon was brought to Alton under heavy guard for his trial, which got underway with jury selection on July 20. A large crowd flocked into Alton for the trial, and a "holiday spirit prevailed," as the regular businesses were so overwhelmed by customers that "temporary refreshment stands" had to be set up on the streets.

The key piece of state evidence presented at the trial, besides Kenyon's original confession, was the match between the second ransom note and the indentations found on his writing pad. The defense countered with two witnesses who testified that Kenyon was at the home of relatives at the time the note was mailed. Several other defense witnesses testified that Kenyon was not normal mentally.

On the evening of July 22, the jury, after deliberating not quite four hours, came back with a guilty verdict and assessed the death penalty. When the verdict was read, Kenyon slumped in his chair and put his arm around Opal, sitting beside him, as she broke into tears. Opal kissed him and hurried away as he was led from the room. A toy pistol modeled from soap was found on his person and taken from him when he got back to his cell. Officers speculated that he had planned to use the fake gun in an attempt to escape.

The next morning, Judge W. E. Barton imposed the death penalty recommended by the jury, sentencing Kenyon to hang on September 2. However, the defense appealed the verdict to the Missouri Supreme Court, automatically staying the execution. Kenyon was transferred to the Butler County Jail at Poplar Bluff for safekeeping until the appeal was decided.

On August 17, 1938, Division II of the Missouri Supreme Court upheld the lower court verdict but remanded the case for resentencing, because, shortly after Kenyon's original execution date, the gas chamber had replaced the gallows as Missouri's official method of carrying out the death penalty. The defense filed a motion for a rehearing of Kenyon's appeal, but the motion was denied on December 20. Kenyon's lawyer then filed a motion to have the petition for a rehearing transferred from Division II to the entire supreme court. This motion, too, was denied on February 21, 1939.

On March 15, Kenyon was escorted from Poplar Bluff to Alton, and Judge Barton resentenced him to death in the gas chamber on April 28. Kenyon was then taken to the state penitentiary in Jefferson City to await execution. A last-minute appeal to a US district judge by Kenyon's counsel for a writ of habeas corpus was overruled two days before the appointed date.

Kenyon spent his final hours reading the Bible, conferring with the prison chaplain, and visiting relatives who called to see him. He entered the gas chamber barely after midnight on April 28 mumbling a psalm and asking for "another talk with the chaplain." The acting warden told him, "I'm sorry, boy, but it's too late," as the steel door of the execution chamber clanged shut behind him. Kenyon was pronounced dead five minutes after the poisonous gas was released, the tenth person to die in Missouri's gas chamber. A large crowd, including Dr. Davis's son and several officials from Howell County, witnessed the execution.

Bibliographic Notes

Chapter One (Rather a Mixed-Up Marriage). The primary sources for this chapter were the *Harrisburg (PA) Telegraph*, September 16, 1866, quoting the *Morgan County (MO) Banner*, and the *Jefferson City Peoples' Tribune*, September 26, 1866, quoting the *Versailles Vindicator*.

Chapter Two (A Remarkable Case of Infatuation). Primary sources include *St. Louis Post Dispatch*, various dates, especially January 18, 1875, January 5, 18, July 30, August 12, September 20, November 12, 1879, July 15, 1881, February 9, March 12, 1882, May 17, 1883; *Indiana State Sentinel*, December 29, 1875; *Cases Argued and Determined in the St. Louis Court of Appeals,* vol. 1, 438-449, vol. 11, 92-104; *Reports of Cases Argued and Determined in the Supreme Court of the State of Missouri*, vol. 64, 591-596; United States Supreme Court Reports, vols. 106, 107, 108, and 109, *Cases Argues and Decided in the Supreme Court of the United States in the October Terms 1881, 1882, and 1883*, 506-517; Kring, *Love and Law in Two Parts.*

Chapter Three (A Devilish Temper and Cruel Disposition). Sources include *History of Randolph and Macon Counties, Missouri*; US Census, 1860, 1870; "The Hade Brown Story;" various newspapers, including *Macon Republican* July 26, 1877, *La Plata Home Press*, July 28, 1877, February 15, 22, December 20, 1879, *Shelbyville Shelby County Herald*, August 1, 1877, *Sedalia Weekly Bazoo*, February 10, 24, May 25, 1880.

Chapter Four (Triple Lynching at Osceola). The author consulted various newspapers for this chapter, especially the

Osceola Sun, May 13, 20, 27, June 10, 1880. See also *Reports of Cases Argued and Determined in the Supreme Court of the State of Missouri*, vol. 81.

Chapter Five (A Case of Patricide?). Sources include various newspapers, including especially the *St. Joseph Weekly Gazette*, September 23, October 28, November 4, 1880, January 27, February 3, 10, March 10, June 2, 30, July 7, 14, 21, 28, 1881; *History of Nodaway County, Mo*; *Reports of Cases Argued and Determined in the Supreme Court of the State of Missouri*, vol. 73.

Chapter Six (Midnight Tragedy in Lucas Place). The primary source for this chapter was the *St. Louis Post-Dispatch*, various dates, including December 19-22, 24, 26, 1881, April 11, 13, 1882.

Chapter Seven (Whiskey and Bad Women). The main sources for this chapter were the *Nevada Daily Mail*, various dates, especially December 27, 28, 1883; the *Sedalia Weekly Bazoo*, especially June 12, December 18, 1883, January 1, 1884; the *Butler Weekly Times*, May 30, 1883, quoting the *Sedalia Bazoo*; and *Reports of Cases Argued and Determined in the Supreme Court of the State of Missouri*, vol. 79.

Chapter Eight (Do You Think It Safe to Kill Them?). The main sources for this chapter were the *Nevada Daily Mail*, numerous dates, including August 7, 10, 20, 22, 24, 26, 28, 29, 31, September 7 1885, January 11, 12, 14, 16, 1886; *Sedalia Weekly Bazoo*, various dates, including December 29, 1885, January 19, June 15, 1886; *Argos (IN) Reflector*, August 20, 1885, January 21, 1886; *St. Louis Post-Dispatch*, January 15, 1886; *History of Vernon County, Missouri*, 367-371; Missouri State Penitentiary Database; *Western Reporter*, vol. 1, 765-766.

Chapter Nine (The Little Chloroformer). Various newspapers, especially the St. Louis Post-Dispatch, April 14, 15,
1885, August 10, 1888; and *Reports of Cases Argued and
Determined in the Supreme Court of the State of Missouri*,
vol. 92, 540-614, were important sources for this chapter.

Chapter Ten (Turlington Tumbles). Principal sources: W. F.
Johnson, *History of Cooper County, Missouri* (Topeka:
Historical Publishing Co., 1919), 348-351; *Reports of Cases
Determined in the Supreme Court of the State of Missouri*,
vol. 102, 642-664; *Sedalia Weekly Bazoo*, various dates,
especially June 24, July 15, 22, August 5, November 18,
1890, March 10, 1891; *St. Louis Post-Dispatch*, November
14, 1890; *Nashville Tennessean*, November 21, 1890, March
8, 1891.

Chapter Eleven (A Fitting End to a Dastardly Career).
Sources include various newspapers, especially the *Chilli-
cothe Constitution-Tribune*, May 30, June 1, 1890; *Sedalia
Weekly Bazoo*, June 3, 10, 17, 1890, February 10, November
3, 1891; *St. Louis Post Dispatch,* May 27, 1890, October 31,
1891; *Chicago Tribune*, March 24, 1867, March 26, 1867,
quoting *Peoria Democrat,* March 23, 1867; *Bloomington (IL)
Pantagraph*, March 27, 1879; US Census, 1850, 1860;
Missouri Marriages; Illinois Civil War Muster and
Descriptive Rolls Database, www.ilsos.gov; *Reports of Cases
Determined in the Supreme Court of the State of Missouri*,
vol. 106, 162-174.

Chapter Twelve (The Death of Lula Noel). Sources: J. A.
Sturges, *History of McDonald County, Missouri (*Pineville,
MO), 1897; various newspapers, including *Neosho Times*,
December 22, 1892, June 8, 1893, December 7, 1894,
Pineville News, December 23, 1892, *Springfield Democrat*,
June 13, December 10, 1893, *St. Louis Post-Dispatch*,
December 21, 29, 1892, June 6, 1893; US Census, 1880;

Reports of Cases Determined in the Supreme Court of the State of Missouri, vol. 124, 443-446.

Chapter Thirteen (Go In or Have Blood). The following newspapers were important sources for this chapter: *Palmyra Spectator*, various dates including October 11, 18, 1894, April 11, 1895, February 28, 1896; *Palmyra Marion County Herald,* March 5, 1896; *St. Louis Post-Dispatch*, April 11, 1895. See also *Reports of Cases Determined in the Supreme Court of the State of Missouri*, vol. 132, 184-199.

Chapter Fourteen (The Tramp Became a Demon). The *St. Louis Post-Dispatch*, September 3, 4, 1896, and the *Sedalia Democrat*, December 15, 1896, were among the main sources for this chapter.

Chapter Fifteen (They Want Me to Say Yes). Main sources: *Macon Republican*, various dates, especially May 27, July 1, 1898; *Macon Times*, August 2, 1895; *Shelbyville Shelby County Herald*, August 3, 1895; *General History of Macon County, Missouri,* vol. 1, 217-220.

Chapter Sixteen (Quiet, Effective Work of the Benevolent Society). The main sources for this chapter were the *Kansas City Journal*, September 12, 13, 1898; *Mexico (MO) Weekly Ledger*, September 15, 1898; US Census, 1900.

Chapter Seventeen (Most Atrocious Crime in Dunklin County History). Among the principal sources for this chapter were the *St. Louis Post Dispatch*, April 26, 1899, July 8, 1900; *Cairo (IL) Citizen*, November 9, 1899; *Sedalia Democrat*, January 18, 1901; *Kennett Dunklin County Democrat*, various dates, especially April 28, 1899, February 22, 1901; *St. Louis Republic*, February 18, 1901; *Reports of Cases Determined in the Supreme Court of the State of Missouri*, vol. 159, 354-381.

Chapter Eighteen (Tragedy of the Tenderloin District). Various newspapers, including the *Poplar Bluff Republican*, October 24, 1901, February 5, 1903; *Poplar Bluff Citizen*, October 24, 1901; *Poplar Bluff Daily Republican*, February 6, 1903; *Southwestern Reporter*, vol. 70, 1117.

Chapter Nineteen (A Sunday Lynching at Paris). Various newspapers, including the *St. Louis Republic*, May 25, 26, 1902; *St. Louis Post-Dispatch*, May 25, 1902; *Columbia Professional World*, May 30, 1902; *Monroe City Democrat*, May 1, July 10, 17, 1902.

Chapter Twenty (A Black and White Lynching). *Lexington Intelligencer*, August 9, 16, 1902; *Macon Republican*, August 16, 1902; *Sedalia Weekly Democrat*, August 14, 1902; *St. Louis Republic*, August 13, 1902; Missouri State Penitentiary Database.

Chapter Twenty-One (Most Terrible Deed Ever Committed in Warren County). Important sources include the *Warrenton Herald*, various dates, especially September 2, 1903, March 30, April 6, 20, June 22, 29, 1904; *Philadelphia Inquirer*, March 26, 1904; *St. Louis Post-Dispatch*, January 10, 1907; *St. Louis Republic*, April 1, 1904; *Reports of Cases Determined in the Supreme Court of the State of Missouri*, vol. 199, 605-640.

Chapter Twenty-Two (Mystery of Pine Flat). Sources: Haddock, "The Riddle of the Phantom Light," *Front Page Detective* (March 1941), 26-31, 48; Missouri State Penitentiary Database; *Houston Herald*, various dates, including February 12, 19, April 29, 1920; *Springfield Republican*, February 11, 12, April 23, 1920; *Springfield Leader and Press*, February 22, April 15, 1920; *Kansas Trails*, "Kiowa County Kansas Woman Was Slain."

Chapter Twenty-Three (For God's Sake, Give Me a Chance). Sources include the *Springfield Leader*, August 13, 1925; *Springfield Republican*, August 8, 1925; *Harrisburg (PA) Evening News*, August 8, 1925; *Chillicothe Constitution-Tribune*, August 7, 1925; *Murphysboro (IL) Daily Independent*, August 8, 1925.

Chapter Twenty-Four (Comin' to No Good End). Sources: *Jefferson City Post-Tribune*, various dates, including January 27, February 3, 4, 1937, April 28, 1939; Bob Hinds, "The Disappearance of Dr. Davis," *West Plains Daily Quill*, September 24, 2016; *St. Louis Post-Dispatch*, January 27, 30, February 1, 1937; *St. Louis Star & Times*, February 3, 1937; *Sedalia Democrat*, July 23, 1937, August 17, 1938; "Troop G History--Missouri State Highway Patrol;" Casetext. State v. Kenyon.

Bibliography

Casetext. "State v. Kenyon," 343 Mo. 1168 (Mo. 1939). https://casetext.com/case/state-v-kenyon-15.

Cases Argued and Determined in the St. Louis Court of Appeals of the State of Missouri from January 10, 1876 to April 10, 1876, vol. 1. A. Moore Berry, Reporter. St. Louis: Soule, Thomas & Wentworth, 1877;

Cases Determined in the St. Louis Court of Appeals of the State of Missouri from July 5, 1881 to March 21, 1882, vol. 11. A. Moore Berry, Reporter. St. Louis: Nixon-Jones Printing Co., 1883.

General History of Macon County, Missouri, vol. 1. Edgar White, ed. Chicago: Henry Taylor & Co., 1910.

"The Hade Brown Story." Lisa Perry, Compiler. http://www.rootsweb.ancestry.com/~momonroe/hadebrown.htm

Haddock, Hugh V. "The Riddle of the Phantom Light." *Front Page Detective.* March 1941.

History of Nodaway County, Mo. St. Joseph, MO: National Historical Co., 1882.

History of Randolph and Macon Counties, Missouri. St Louis: National Historical Company, 1884.

History of Vernon County, Missouri. 1887. Reprint, Clinton (MO): the Printery, 1974.

Illinois Civil War Muster and Descriptive Rolls Database. https://www.ilsos.gov/isaveterans/civilmustersrch.jsp.

Johnson, W. F. *History of Cooper County, Missouri.* Topeka: Historical Publishing Co., 1919.

Kansas Trails. "Kiowa County, Kansas Woman Was Slain." http://genealogytrails.com/kan/kiowa/rosenberger.html.

Kring, Charles F. *Love and Law in Two Parts: The Only True History of the Killing of Mrs. Dora C. J. Broemser*. St. Louis: The Author, 1882.

Missouri Marriages. https://search.ancestry.com/search/db.aspx?dbid=1171.

Missouri State Penitentiary Database. Missouri State Archives. https://s1.sos.mo.gov/records/archives/archivesdb/msp/.

Reports of Cases Argued and Determined in the Supreme Court of the State of Missouri, vol. 64. Truman A. Post, Reporter. St. Louis: W. I. Gilbert, 1877.

Reports of Cases Argued and Determined in the Supreme Court of the State of Missouri, vol. 73. Thomas K. Skinker, Reporter. Kansas City: Ramsey, Millett & Hudson, 1881.

Reports of Cases Argued and Determined in the Supreme Court of the State of Missouri, vol. 79. Thomas K. Skinker, Reporter. Kansas City: Ramsey, Millett and Hudson, 1884.

Reports of Cases Argued and Determined in the Supreme Court of the State of Missouri, vol. 81. F. M. Brown, Reporter. Kansas City: Ramsey, Millett and Hudson, 1885.

Reports of Cases Argued and Determined in the Supreme Court of the State of Missouri, vol. 92. F. M. Brown, Reporter. Columbia, MO: E. W. Stephens, 1888.

Reports of Cases Determined in the Supreme Court of the State of Missouri, vol. 102. F. M. Brown, Reporter. Columbia, MO: E. W. Stephens, 1891.

Reports of Cases Determined in the Supreme Court of the State of Missouri, vol. 106, F. M. Brown, Reporter. Columbia, MO: E. W. Stephens, 1892.

Reports of Cases Determined in the Supreme Court of the State of Missouri, vol. 124. F. M. Brown, Reporter. Columbia, MO: E. W. Stephens, 1895.

Reports of Cases Determined in the Supreme Court of the State of Missouri, vol. 132. F. M. Brown, Reporter, Columbia, MO: E. W. Stephens, 1896.

Reports of Cases Determined in the Supreme Court of the State of Missouri, vol. 159. Perry S. Rader, Reporter. Columbia, MO: E. W. Stephens, 1901.

Reports of Cases Determined in the Supreme Court of the State of Missouri, vol. 199. Perry S. Rader, Reporter. Columbia, MO: E. W. Stephens, 1907.

Southwestern Reporter, vol. 70, November 19, 1902-January 7, 1903. St. Paul: West Publishing Company, 1903.

Sturges, J. A. *History of McDonald County, Missouri.* Pineville, MO, 1897.

Troop G History--Missouri State Highway Patrol," https://www.mshp.dps.missouri.gov/MSHPWeb/ PatrolDivisions/TroopHeaduarters/TroopG/ documents/TroopGHistory001.pdf.

United States Census, 1850, 1860, 1870, 1880, 1900. www.familysearch.org.

United States Supreme Court Reports, vols. 106, 107, 108, and 109. *Cases Argued and Decided in the Supreme Court of the United States in the October Terms 1881, 1882, and 1883.* Stephen K. Williams, Recorder. Rochester, NY: The Lawyers' Cooperative Publishing Co., 1885.

Western Reporter, vol. 1. Robert Destry, ed. Rochester (NY): The Lawyers' Co-operative Publishing Co., 1885.

Index

Allen, Lou, 56, 57, 59, 60

Alton, Missouri, 204, 205

Andrew County Jail, 49

Archer, Tom, 63, 66, 67, 73

Arkoe, Missouri, 40

Auckland, New Zealand, 86, 88, 89

Ava, Missouri, 198

Bacon, W. W., 115, 116

Baily, Ephraim, 39

Baily, Isam, 39

Baker, Samuel, 195

Ball, Claude R., 178, 179, 180

Barham, W. T., 151

Barker, Jack, 38, 39

Barton, W. E., 204, 205

Belvidere, Kansas, 185

Bernie, Missouri, 146, 151

Bishop, Etta, 76

Bitler, Samuel (aka Gilbert Hall), 184, 185, 186, 187, 188, 189

Blackwell, Horace F., 171

Blanton, Horace H., 82, 83

Bohon, William, 35

Boonville, Missouri, 94, 95, 96, 99, 100, 102, 110, 173, 181, 183

Bowen, Ed, 154, 155

Boyle, J. G., 60

Brenicke, August, 105, 106

Brighton, Jonas V., 44, 45, 46, 47, 48, 50, 51, 52

Brighton, Virginia, 44, 47, 48

Brixey, Buster, 197, 202

Broemser, Amanda, 16

Broemser, Dora, 11, 12, 13, 14, 15, 16, 17, 18, 20, 21

Broemser, Jacob, 12, 14, 15, 16, 18

Brooks, Hugh Mottram (aka Walter H. Lennox-Maxwell, aka T. C. D'Auquier), 85, 86, 87, 88, 89, 90, 91, 92
Browitt, Ann, 134
Browitt, Annie, 134
Browitt, Ethel, 134
Brown, Hade, 23, 24, 27, 28, 29, 30, 31, 32, 33
Brown, Martha, 26
Brown, Sarah, 24
Brown, Susan, 23, 24, 27, 28, 29, 30, 31, 32, 33
Buchanan County Jail, 49
Buescher, Daniel, 173, 176
Buescher, Fritz, 176
Buffalo, New York, 175
Burckhartt, G. H., 28, 29
Burke, John, 85, 86, 87
Burton, Charles G., 68, 80
Butler County Jail, 157, 205
Cabool, Missouri, 184, 186, 187, 188
Cairo, Missouri, 23, 26
Carthage, Missouri, 81
Case, Missouri, 174, 175, 177
Casteel, B. Marvin, 198
Chicago, Illinois, 15, 129, 175
Church, William E., 173, 174, 175, 176, 177, 178, 179, 180, 181, 182, 183
Clark, James W., 160, 163, 164, 166
Clark, Pearl, 152, 153, 154, 155, 156
Clark, Steve, 152, 153, 154, 155, 156, 157
Cleveland, Grover, 89
Cleveland, Ohio, 175
Clifton, Robert W., 187
Clinton, Missouri, 38
Cofer, J. J., 115
Collins, George, 178
Cooper County Jail, 94, 95, 98, 99
Cowskin Creek, 111, 113
Cranmer, Thomas C., 95, 96

Craven, John F., 191, 194, 195
Crittenden, Thomas, 50, 51, 53
Cummins, Raymond, 191, 192, 194, 195
Curry, Hiram, 38, 39
Dale, May, 188
Danville, Missouri, 127, 130
Davis, J. C. B., 196, 197, 198, 199, 200, 202, 205
Dawson, Lafe, 47
Dawson, Maggie, 153, 154, 155
Delventhal, J. W., 176
Dixon, William, 128, 129, 130
Dockery, A. M., 150, 156, 157, 176
Dora, Missouri, 200, 202
Dove, A. N., 188
Drake, Lyman, 181
Duncan, G. W., 187
Dunklin County Jail, 148, 149
East Albany, New York, 132
Eby, David, 163, 166
Edelen, J. E., 114, 116
Elliott, Frank, 184, 186, 187, 188
Emerson, Tom, 36
Excelsior Springs, Missouri, 190, 191, 192, 193, 194, 195
Fisher, Belle, 30, 31
Fisher, William, 69, 72
Fleming, Jacob, 35
Folk, Joseph W., 183
Fort Scott, Kansas, 75, 77
Fort, James L., 149, 155
Four Courts Jail, 60, 98, 178
Fox, Delilah, 64
Fox, Milton, 64, 71
Fox, William, 63, 64, 65, 66, 67, 68, 69, 70, 71, 72, 73, 74, 75
Francis, David R., 109
Frommell, Geraldine, 196
Galena, Kansas, 75

Gallagher, Ed, 176, 177
Gammon, Alice, 127, 128, 129, 130, 131
Garber, J. B., 175, 176, 177, 179, 180
Gates, Harry, 167, 168, 169, 170, 171
Gatlin, Will, 156, 157
Gilbert, William, 36
Glenn, A. J., 137
Gore, Missouri, 177
Graham, R. E., 180
Gregory, Milo, 149, 150
Grimes, Decatur, 38, 39
Grimmet, Missouri, 198, 199, 201
Grow, Mary Belle, 159
Grow, Stephen, 159, 160, 163, 164, 165
Grow, William, 158, 159, 160, 161, 162, 164
Guggenmoos, Otto, 172
Hannibal, Missouri, 64, 65
Harding, John, 154, 155
Harryman, W. D., 39
Hartly, Cal, 39
Harwood, Missouri, 79
Hensley, Wes, 94, 95, 96, 99
Higgins, Lou, 66
Hill, H. W., 194
Hill, William W., 82, 83
Holly, Laura, 111, 112, 113, 117
Holly, Sidney, 112, 113, 117
Holt, Charles N., 190, 192
Holt, Maud, 190, 191, 192
Horn, Olga, 133, 134
Hornbeck, Albert, 100, 101
Houston, Missouri, 188, 189
Howard, Thomas, 63, 64, 65, 66, 67, 68, 69, 70, 71, 73, 74, 75
Howell County Jail, 204
Howell, John C., 48
Hughes, Mary, 120, 121, 122

Hunnewell, Missouri, 159, 161
Huntsville, Missouri, 27, 29, 33
Jackson County Jail, 200
Jackson, Missouri, 148
Jefferson City, Missouri, 51, 68, 81, 83, 98, 99, 119, 189, 205
Jewett, O. L., 166
Jobe, Anderson, 117
Johnson City, Missouri, 35
Johnson, George, 168, 169, 170, 171
Johnson, Mrs. Henry, 159, 161
Jones, Benjamin, 141, 142, 143
Jones, Mit C., 143
Jones, William C., 18
Joplin, Missouri, 111, 112, 113, 115, 116
Kane, J. J., 132
Kansas City, Missouri, 30, 33, 82, 167, 186, 194, 195, 200, 201, 204
Kansas State Penitentiary, 44, 47, 189
Kennett, Missouri, 148, 149
Kenyon, Robert, 199, 200, 201, 202, 204, 205
Kenyon, Samuel, 198, 201
Kenyon, Sophie, 201
Kern, Jake, 154, 155
Kimball, E. E., 63, 68, 69
King, David, 28
Koch, Charles, 104
Koechel, John, 135
Kring, Charles F., 11, 12, 13, 14, 15, 16, 17, 18, 19, 20, 21, 22
Kring, Emma, 12
Kring, Frederick, 12
Kring, Margaret, 12, 13, 14, 15, 17, 18, 21, 22
Lanagan, Missouri, 111, 113, 114, 116, 117
Landgraf, Henry, 91
Larkin, Tom, 127, 128, 129, 130, 131, 132
Laughlin, Henry, 19, 20
Laws, Lewis A., 175, 176, 178

Lawson, Missouri, 190, 191
Lefever, Harriet, 7, 8, 9
Leubke, Amelia, 135, 136
Leubke, Ann, 135
Leubke, Bertha, 135
Lewis, Ed, 153, 154, 155
Lexington, Missouri, 167, 168, 169, 170, 171
Liberty, Missouri, 141, 142, 143, 191
Lost Creek, 174
Lundy, J. M., 73, 74
Lynch, John, 177
Macon County Jail, 135
Macon, Missouri, 133, 134, 135, 136, 138, 139, 140, 179
Madison, Missouri, 33
Malden, Missouri, 145, 146, 148
Maloney, Mollie, 57
Marceline, Missouri, 136
Marion County Jail, 125
Marmaduke, John S., 81, 89
Marmaton River, 77, 79, 80
Martindale, E. C., 80
Maryville, Missouri, 40, 41, 42, 45, 48, 49, 50, 51, 54
Matlock, Nicholas, 33
McAllister, Frank, 160, 161, 162, 166
McCaskill, Jack, 187, 188
McCullough, John, 89, 90
Memphis, Tennessee, 107, 136, 185
Miller, Mary, 158, 162
Miller, Samuel, 21, 22
Minor, Samuel, 120, 121
Missouri Supreme Court, 19, 20, 22, 29, 39, 40, 49, 69, 80, 91, 97, 98, 100, 108, 109, 119, 124, 145, 149, 150, 155, 183, 204, 205
Mitchell, E. Y., 38
Mitchell, Walter, 191, 192, 193, 194, 195
Mitchell, Wilford, 41, 44, 45, 47, 49, 50, 51, 52, 54
Moberly House of Refuge, 173

Moberly, Missouri, 26, 27, 33
Monroe County Jail, 161
Montgomery, Annie, 141, 144
Montgomery, Emma, 141
Montgomery, James, 141
Moore, Arimenta, 64
Moore, Charles, 105, 106
Moore, Jeff, 103, 105, 106, 109
Morehouse, Stephen, 45
Morsey, William, 172
Moundville, Missouri, 64, 65
Mud Creek (St. Libory), Illinois, 14, 21
Mulcahy, Kitty, 56, 57, 59, 60, 61, 62
Mulkey, Mattie, 83
Myrick, Missouri, 167
Nashville, Illinois, 15
Nashville, Tennessee, 94
Neeleyville, Missouri, 149
Nelson, John, 120, 121, 122, 123, 124, 125, 126
Nelson, Lavinia, 120, 121, 122, 123, 125
Neosho, Missouri, 112, 116, 117
Nevada, Missouri, 63, 64, 65, 67, 68, 70, 71, 72, 75, 77, 79, 81, 82, 83
New London, Missouri, 120, 123, 125
New York, New York, 76, 129
Newton County Jail, 116
Nichols, Saphronia, 136
Nodaway County Jail, 45, 48, 52
Noel, Lula, 111, 112, 113, 114, 115, 116, 117, 118, 119
Noel, Missouri, 112
Noel, Susan, 112
Noel, William, 112, 114
North Fork River, 197, 198, 199
Olden, Missouri, 199, 202
Osage River, 8
Osborn, Nanetta, 75, 77, 78, 79, 80, 81, 82, 83, 84
Osborne, Mary, 25, 26, 27

Osceola, Missouri, 34, 35, 36, 38, 39
Otterville, Missouri, 93, 100
Palmyra, Missouri, 123, 125, 126
Paris, Missouri, 159, 160, 161, 163, 165, 166
Parkinson, John D., 38, 39
Parks, John, 35, 36, 37, 38
Parrish, J. C., 23, 24, 25, 26, 30
Parrish, Lutie, 25, 26
Parrish, Martha, 23, 24, 25, 26, 30
Peoria, Illinois, 188
Pettis County Jail, 95, 105, 108
Phelps, John S., 38
Philadelphia, Pennsylvania, 175, 176, 177
Pierce, Chesley, 35, 36, 37, 38
Pineville, Missouri, 112, 116
Polster, George, 176, 177, 178
Poplar Bluff, Missouri, 149, 152, 153, 156, 205
Powers, John, 55
Prater, Henry, 116
Pratt, Ed, 126
Preller, Charles Arthur, 85, 86, 87, 88, 89, 90, 91
Pryor Creek, Indian Territory, 94, 96
Ralls County Jail, 123
Ramsey, W. W., 51
Randolph County Jail, 27, 29, 33
Randolph, Missouri, 141, 143
Ransom, A. J., 151
Reed Kirk, Susan, 104
Reed, Albert, 186, 188
Reed, Matt, 104
Rhineland, Missouri, 127, 128, 129, 130, 132
Roberts, David C., 141
Rochester, Minnesota, 26
Rockwood, C. A., 79, 80
Roewe, Minnie, 175, 176, 178
Rolla, Missouri, 199, 200
Roman, J. A., 189

Rose, Jane, 63, 64, 65, 66, 67, 70, 71, 73, 74
Rosenberger, Susan, 185
Rowell, Samuel J., 194
Rudolph, Bill "The Missouri Kid", 178
Ryland, John E., 108
Salt River, 158, 159, 164
Salyers, Charles, 167, 168, 169, 170, 171
San Francisco, California, 88, 89
Satterfield, William, 149
Saunders, W. R., 45
Savannah, Missouri, 49, 50
Scharlow, Billy, 56, 57, 58, 59, 60, 62
Scott, George, 187
Scrutchfield, Guthrie, 140
Sedalia, Missouri, 82, 83, 93, 94, 95, 96, 97, 100, 103, 104,
105
Sewell, Evaline, 75
Sewell, Jacob, 75, 77, 79, 80
Sewell, McClure "Mack", 75
Shelton, Nat, 179, 180, 182, 183
Sherwood, Thomas, 20
Shirk, William S., 97, 101
Shockley, Hiram, 9, 10
Simmons, William, 111, 112, 113, 114, 115, 116, 117, 118,
119
Slocum, Elijah, 7, 8, 9, 10
Smith, Ellis, 106, 107, 110
Smith, John, 35, 36, 37, 38
Smith, Smith, 35
Snell, Claud E., 163
Springfield, Missouri, 188
St. Clair County Jail, 34, 35, 36
St. Joseph, Missouri, 49, 52, 54
St. Louis, Missouri, 12, 13, 15, 16, 22, 26, 27, 29, 55, 85, 86,
88, 89, 98, 99, 148, 149, 175, 177, 178, 179, 201
St. Paul, Minnesota, 175, 191
Stair, Frederick, 76, 81, 82

Stair, Henry S., 75, 76, 77, 78, 79, 80, 81, 82, 83, 84
Stogsdill, Dick, 187
Stratton, D. P., 63, 68, 69
Stull, John, 120, 121, 122, 123
Stull, Mary, 121
Stull, Willie, 121, 123, 124, 125
Talbott, Albert P. "Bud", 40, 41, 42, 43, 44, 45, 46, 47, 48, 49, 50, 52, 53, 54
Talbott, Belle, 41, 44, 45, 46, 51, 53
Talbott, Ed, 40, 43, 45, 46, 47, 48, 49, 50, 52, 53, 54
Talbott, Perry H., 41, 42, 43, 44, 45, 46, 47, 49, 51, 52, 53, 54
Talbott, William, 48
Temple, Andy, 93, 94, 95, 96
Tettaton, George, 148, 150
Tettaton, James Henry, 145, 146, 147, 148, 149, 150, 151
Tettaton, Jane, 145, 146, 147, 148, 149
Tettaton, Washington, 146
Texas County Jail, 188, 189
Thomas, Oscar, 167, 169, 171
Toel, Henry, 45, 46, 47, 53
Trimble, Mary, 64, 69
Triplett. William, 35
Tucker, Ewing, 7, 8, 9, 10
Turlington, Ann, 96
Turlington, John Oscar, 93, 94, 95, 96, 97, 98, 99, 100, 101, 102, 110
Turner, Charles, 56
Utt, Leonard, 190, 191
Vernon County Jail, 68, 79, 81
Warrenton, Missouri, 172, 175, 176, 178, 179, 183
Weaver, Charles, 123
Webb City, Missouri, 113
Welch, Opal, 200, 201, 202, 204
West Plains, Missouri, 197, 198, 200, 204
Whitecotton, James H., 163, 164
Williams, Henry, 133, 134, 135, 136, 137, 138, 140

Williamson, Milton, 107

Williamson, Thomas, 103, 104, 105, 106, 107, 108, 109, 110

Willow Springs, Missouri, 196, 197, 198, 199, 200, 202

Witherup, Abraham, 158, 159, 160, 161, 162, 163, 164, 165, 166

Wyatt, Henry, 40, 41, 45, 46, 47, 49, 50, 51, 52, 53, 54

Yeater, Henriette "Nettie", 173, 174, 175, 177

Yeater, Henry, 172, 173, 175, 177, 178

Young, Callie, 173, 178

Young, John E. "Jack", 175, 176, 177, 178, 183

About the Author

Larry Wood is a retired public schoolteacher and freelance writer specializing in the history of Missouri and the Ozarks. He has published fifteen books on regional history and two historical novels. His numerous stories and articles have appeared in journals and magazines ranging from the *Missouri Historical Review* to *Wild West Magazine*. An honorary lifetime member of the Missouri Writers' Guild, Wood maintains a blog on Missouri and Ozarks history at www.ozarks-history.blogspot.com. He and his wife, Gigi, live in Joplin, Missouri.

Printed in Great Britain
by Amazon